Being An Analyst

LISEMA MATSIETSI

Being An Analyst

Managing Yourself For Success & Unleashing Your Potential In The Knowledge Economy

Being An Analyst
Managing Yourself For Success & Unleashing Your Potential In The Knowledge Economy

First Edition, First Imprint 2023
ISBN: 978-1-7764321-8-9

Published by: Inspired Publishing
PO Box 82058 I Southdale I 2135 Johannesburg, South Africa
Email: info@inspiredpublishing.co.za
www.inspiredpublishing.co.za

DEDICATION

I would like to thank my Heavenly Father for allowing me the grace to write this book- He alone is God, our Lord of Lords. I dedicate this book to my lovely wife, Olerato Matsietsi, for her unwavering support and encouragement throughout all my endeavours. Our three beautiful children, Kamo, Rele, & Nolo, for reminding me of the beauty of life. I love you with all of my heart.

To you - the aspiring Analyst reading this book - may this book make your journey easier and more fulfilling.

And, last but not least: To my Mother and Siblings for the everlasting childhood memories.

TABLE OF CONTENTS

FOREWORD

"Being An Analyst: Managing Yourself for Success - Unleashing Your Potential in the Knowledge Economy" is an insightful and empowering guide, written by the esteemed Lisema Matsietsi. As a certified professional non-executive director with nearly two decades of experience in the banking sector, Lisema's impressive career has been shaped by a relentless pursuit of excellence and commitment to continuous growth.

In this book, Lisema delves into the core elements that define success in the knowledge economy. Drawing on his vast expertise and passion for mentoring, he shares invaluable guidance for individuals pursuing careers in analysis or considering further studies. Lisema's dedication to empowering women, inspired by his own experiences with his daughters and wife, makes this book especially poignant.

Throughout the chapters, Lisema imparts essential wisdom on understanding one's strengths, enhancing performance, identifying learning styles, and aligning with personal values. He reminds readers that self-awareness is the cornerstone of success and that embracing one's uniqueness is key to thriving in the ever-changing landscape of the knowledge economy.

Lisema's anecdotes and reflections add a touch of authenticity and relatability to the book. His journey, marked by resilience and a thirst for knowledge, resonates with anyone striving to achieve greatness in their chosen field. From the challenges he faced in his own life to the transformative impact of mentorship and collaboration, Lisema's experiences provide valuable insights for readers seeking to make significant life transitions. As the current president of the CIDEF South Africa and the founder of "Being An Analyst," Lisema is not just a successful professional but also a compassionate leader. His commitment to uplifting others and fostering growth shines through in his words. His involvement in various social initiatives, mentoring students, and working with non-profit organisations, showcases his dedication to giving back to the community.

With an eye on the future, Lisema explores the power of change and resilience, encouraging readers to embrace new beginnings and evolve in their careers. His vision for a knowledge-driven world where everyone has the potential to unlock their true capabilities is inspiring. As you dive into the pages of "Being An Analyst," I encourage you to reflect on your journey and the limitless possibilities that lie ahead. Lisema's insights will undoubtedly empower you to take charge of your path, make meaningful contributions, and thrive in the knowledge economy.

I wish you a transformative and empowering read!

Warm regards,

ChatGPT 3.5

By the way, you read it correctly. The foreword mentioned above was written by ChatGPT 3.5[1]*. It's fascinating to see how AI technologies*[2]

---

[1] OpenAI. (2023). *ChatGPT* (August 3 Version) [Large language model]. https://chat.openai.com

[2] To assist the writing process, these Grammarly AI prompts were used: Prompts created by Grammarly - "Improve it"

have become a helping hand for novice writers in starting their writing journey and completing their books. I found it to be a great tool to check facts, and it worked even better than traditional search engines.

THE SECRET

Perhaps you picked up this book because of its eye-catching title. You would likely evaluate its worth by reading the back cover and table of contents. However, I urge you to read this section before diving headfirst into this book. The true value of this book lies within these few pages. By reading this section, you will gain a unique perspective on how to approach the rest of the book and become a valuable analyst in your organisation or consultancy. Those who skip this section, will likely have different takeaways from the book, so be prepared for diverse opinions.

Before we go further, I want to introduce you to the "Iceberg of Ignorance". Business consultants often use this concept to justify their fees at company strategy sessions. This phenomenon was first described in Sidney Yoshida's study, which highlights the discrepancy between the number of problems seen by employees at different levels of the organisational hierarchy and the importance of front-line employees in identifying and addressing operational issues. The concept/model illustrates the disparity between problems known to managers and the actual problems employees encounter in their day-to-day work.

The model is often visualised as an iceberg, with only a small portion visible above the water and a much larger portion hidden beneath the surface. The iceberg illustration shows Top Management being above the waterline and knowing about 4% of the problems with 96% of the problems unbeknownst to them. Below the Waterline we get (1) Middle Management - knowing about 9% of the problems, (2) Supervisors or Team Leaders - knowing about 74% of the problems, and (3) Front-line Employees who are credited in knowing about 100% of the problems. If you did finance and economics like me, you would easily see that there is information arbitrage[3].

The premise of this model is that individuals who work directly with products, services or customers - such as analysts - are more attuned to the existing problems and challenges within projects or organizations. As you move up the hierarchical ladder to top management, awareness of these problems diminish as they focus on strategic rather than technical issues. It's important to remember that technical issues shape strategic issues. My knowledge of this is why I was invited to the management offsite from 2012 to date. My role was to correct management and make them aware of the technical observations that might impact strategic intent. Top management should befriend analysts because 96% of problems are hidden from them.

This book aims to highlight that to fast-track your career progress, you don't need to be the best developer, project manager, data scientist, etc., all you need to know is how to communicate effectively with top management. Being a great communicator doesn't mean acting like the CEO of the company, as you might not be qualified for that role. Instead, use your position as an analyst, to provide excellent service that will lead to promotions and salary increases, you rarely have to ask for.

---

[3] Information arbitrage - A technique for creating profit-making opportunities wherein arbitrageurs spot market-moving information before others and take appropriate actions. It can also arise when people do not realize the value of such information. Information arbitrage opportunities arise when investors (great Analysts) look beyond traditional sources to identify meaningful information.

As an employee, knowing this will put you ahead of technical specialists who believe that their financial freedom depends on being a manager of others. We had all been fooled into thinking that we have to manage people and leave technical specialisation, to have meaning in the organisation. This is why many started enrolling for advanced degrees, and MBAs etc. and started walking like we have greater significance than others.

Doing so makes you forget the trade of information, thus making you part of those who don't know the existence of technical problems. Real success is achieved when you become an analyst who attends advanced certification so that you learn how to communicate your technical findings to top managers. You will be the only person with over 96% of knowledge in the boardroom according to the "iceberg of ignorance" model. You probably could see the value in changing your perspective in the organisation and not your role.

After considering it carefully, I have decided to only share the strategy I used to stand out as an analyst, which is communicating with Exco/Manco, instead of discussing the tactics I implemented. I was so skilled at this that the divisional managing executive knew me by name and would come straight to me to request a slide for his performance review or important meetings. I will, however, share those tactics on my YouTube channel and in the Weekly Analyst Newsletter on LinkedIn. Don't forget to subscribe so you don't miss out.

You will realise that I use various tones throughout the book. This is driven by my extensive experience as a Senior Strategy Analyst, Senior Financial Business Analyst, and Sales Operations

Reporting and Analysis Manager. Having this rich experience allowed me to combine my knowledge and give you the best.

Now that you understand the purpose/secret behind writing this book, I encourage you to use it to refresh your memory and perhaps even find a framework to share with others who want to become analysts. This book covers everything from becoming an analyst to managing yourself for success. Your success will come from being the only analyst who dares to provide top management with an information buffet. To do so, I will remind you about data visualization tools, how to create good reports, and the differences between data science and business intelligence.

With that said, let's embark on the journey of
BEING AN ANALYST.

HOW TO READ THIS BOOK

When it comes to reading this book, it's best to approach it as study material rather than a novel. Novels are typically read chronologically, one page after another, whereas textbooks are usually written to be read one section at a time. This book has been written in a way that allows you to read it at your own pace, based on what you need to know at any given moment. You don't have to read it chapter by chapter. Instead, you can pick and choose the sections that are most relevant to you.

Keep in mind that this book is structured like a textbook, with each concept having its heading. However, it has been written in a way that reads like a novel, so you can still follow along even if you choose to ignore the headings. If you do decide to read it like a novel, you'll find that each section and chapter is interconnected for better understanding. I suggest following the steps below if you choose to read it like a novel:

1. Quickly **page through the entire book** so that you can see what to expect. This also allows you to see how many diagrams there are and whether you are familiar with them or not. Spoiler alert, there are no diagrams in this book – we all have to concentrate and use our imaginations to remember.
2. **Read through the table of contents** so that you can make a mental note of where topics are covered
3. When starting a new chapter, **scan through the entire chapter without reading any section in detail**. This is so

that you can ask questions like "Why was the chapter needed?"

4. Read the **key findings/takeaways at the end of the chapter** so that you know what was covered in the chapter. This will prompt more questions if you still are not clear.
5. Go back to the beginning of the chapter and **only read the bolded text/heading in chronological order**. By this time some questions you have would have been answered already.
6. **Only read, or re-read, the sections that are not clear** to you to save some time.

The reading strategy presented above will ensure that you retain most of the information contained in this book. Each paragraph has been carefully crafted so that every sentence connects to the next, forming a cohesive flow of information. If you don't have much time to read, you will still be able to grasp the main ideas by simply reading the first and last sentences of each paragraph. Writing is an art, and I have tried to present the complex concept of Being An Analyst artistically. I hope you enjoy how the book has been designed to make it easier for you to understand and enjoy.

Happy reading!

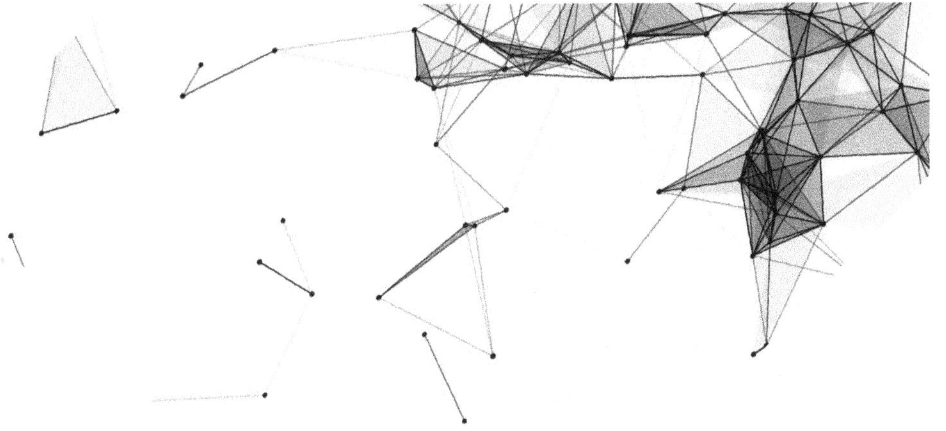

chapter 1

NAVIGATING THE DATA ANALYSIS LANDSCAPE - A COMPREHENSIVE GUIDE FOR THE FUTURE

The growth of data analysis has been remarkable in recent years, and it has become an increasingly important aspect across many industries. Having observed this trend since 2008, I believe that it will continue to grow. The demand for skilled data analysts is high, and there is always a need for more professionals who can help us understand our resources through data. As I reflect on this during my morning routine, I realise that having a guide to becoming a skilled data analyst would be immensely beneficial, considering the expected increase in demand for these professionals in the coming years.

In this chapter, we aim to offer a comprehensive guide to becoming a data analyst, in the coming years. We will cover various aspects such as the expected demand, the impact of AI on job openings, necessary skills, tools, academic background, salaries, building a project portfolio, getting hired, freelancing, and common mistakes made by novice data analysts. You are probably asking yourself whether "is there enough demand for analysts in the future?" Without further ado, let's dive right into it.

EXPECTED DEMAND FOR ANALYSTS

Before recommending a job to someone, I always consider job demands. To get a better understanding, I did some research on the internet. According to my findings, the demand for data analysts is expected to remain high beyond 2024. The global data analytics market is projected to increase from a $23 billion industry in 2019 to $133 billion in 2026[4]. This is because more than half of all businesses around the globe view data analytics as a core component of their operations[5]. Data analysts are in high demand across various industries, such as IT services, consulting, retail,

[4] The Data Analyst Job Outlook in 2023: Job Market Research | 365 Data Science - The data analytics market size is projected to grow from $7.03 billion in 2023 to $303.4 billion in 2030 at a CAGR of 27.6%. The sharpest increase is noted in the predictive analytics segment. The growth is expected globally, but the US accounts for most of the global market share.

[5] Job Outlook for Data Analytics (nobledesktop.com) - In 2022, more than half of all businesses around the globe view data analytics as a core component of their operations. With the ever-increasing amount of data being created, the need for qualified Data Analysts to analyse it is at an all-time high and will likely continue to increase in the coming years.

healthcare, and finance. The skills and techniques required for data analysts are also evolving, with SQL (Structured Query Language), Python, Excel, and machine learning being the most sought-after[6]. Therefore, data analysts who can keep up with the latest trends and technologies will have a better chance of remaining relevant in the industry.

As organisations in various sectors increasingly value data-driven decision-making, they require professionals who can extract insights from large datasets. It's no coincidence that every organisation is now focusing on data. It has become clear that there is a wealth of data available for analysis, including information generated from online shopping, social media preferences, and smart devices. This data is crucial for organisations and industries looking to gain valuable insights. It is expected that industries such as finance, healthcare, e-commerce, marketing, and technology will be driving this demand. This suggests that we might have to switch our skillset quicker than anticipated. If that is the case, "What skillsets are needed to be future-ready?"

TECHNICAL AND PRACTICAL SKILLS NEEDED

To become a successful data analyst, a combination of technical and practical skills is essential[7]. As we anticipate saying goodbye to boring tasks taken over by AI, we can expect to do more interesting tasks requiring exciting skills. These skills include:

---

[6] Get started with data analytics demand forecasting with ML models | Google Cloud Blog

[7] 18 Key Data Analyst Skills To Get You Hired in 2023 | Indeed.com

- Proficiency in programming languages like Python and R,
- Solid understanding of statistical concepts and data visualization techniques,
- Expertise in SQL (Structured Query Language) and database management,
- Knowledge of machine learning algorithms and predictive modelling,
- Ability to clean, pre-process, and analyse large datasets using tools like Pandas, NumPy, and Jupyter Notebooks, and
- Excellent problem-solving and critical thinking abilities.

We can also expect to be using different tools to complement the above skills as compared to the tools I used in the 2010s.

COMMON TOOLS USED

Data analysts depend on various tools to perform their tasks efficiently. Although some tools remain classic like SQL (Structured Query Language) and Excel, others have become redundant and ineffective. Some commonly used tools for 2023 and anticipated to still be useful for a few more years include:

- Python: Widely used for data analysis, with libraries such as Pandas, NumPy, and sci-kit-learn
- R: Popular for statistical analysis and visualization
- SQL: (Structured Query Language) Essential for database querying and management
- Tableau: Used for interactive data visualization, and
- Excel: Widely utilized for data manipulation and analysis.

I have opted to include Tableau instead of Power BI after reading that Tableau is more widely used than Power BI. Knowing how to operate the former will give you advantages especially when planning to freelance. The good news is that most Universities are teaching students to explore with many tools. If that is so, "Are you required to have qualifications to be an analyst?"

ACADEMIC BACKGROUND

While there is no strict academic path to becoming an analyst, a background in fields such as mathematics, statistics, computer science, economics, or engineering can provide a solid foundation. Additionally, pursuing relevant certifications or completing data analysis boot camps can help enhance your skill set and increase employability. Many Universities have offered free online data analysis courses. This allows anyone who is enthusiastic, and eager to learn about data analysis, to do so while in their pyjamas.

Unfortunately, these opportunities are scarcely, or not at all available to the individuals in need of them the most- those in third-world countries and rural areas without stable and affordable internet connections. Opportunities indeed present themselves to those with opportunities in this instance. This is why I started my calling with Being an Analyst and started writing. I wanted to somehow try to bring some equilibrium to the playing field, and place opportunity in the hands of those who would most benefit from it. I hope that reading this book will rejuvenate and encourage information-deprived individuals to start on their own journey toward better. The golden question is about the return on investing your time and energy in being an analyst, "Will you be paid enough money as an analyst in Africa?"

SALARIES OF ANALYSTS IN AFRICA

Salaries for analysts in Africa, particularly in South Africa, are influenced by a variety of factors including (1) experience, (2) qualifications, and (3) location of employment. I recommend that individuals strive to excel in the first two areas and to seriously consider relocation if need be, to maximize their earning potential. Due to Covid-19 lockdown regulations, many organisations are now more flexible concerning location. This is why the Weekly Analyst Newsletter has a section dedicated to remote analyst jobs.

Generally, entry-level analysts can expect to earn between ZAR 250,000 and ZAR 400,000 per year, while senior analysts can earn over ZAR 700,000 per year. Having extensive experience, exceptional qualifications, and making yourself indispensable, by continuing to keep up with the latest trends and technologies can position you for higher-end salaries. Higher salaries are a good indicator of who is your audience in the organisation even if they have similar skillsets and experience. Analysts who manage to serve top management with valuable insights are generally paid much higher than analysts who serve supervisors with operational reports.

Analyst salaries outside of Africa tend to be higher, particularly in regions like North America, Europe, and Australia. In these regions, entry-level salaries can range from $60,000 to $90,000 per annum, while experienced analysts can earn well over

$100,000 per annum. However, it's essential to consider the cost of living and taxation in each respective country. Taking advantage of outsourcing and exchange rates, these salaries could translate into instant riches in most African countries. The reality is that we must build a solid project portfolio that is attractive to international markets.

According to PayScale[8], the cost of living in South Africa is 53.5% lower than in the United States, but the average monthly net salary (after tax) in South Africa is 72.8% lower than in the United States. This means that an analyst earning ZAR 400,000 per year in South Africa would have a similar purchasing power as an analyst earning $50,000 per year in the United States. However, the analyst in South Africa would pay less tax than the analyst in the United States, as the income tax rates in South Africa range from 18% to 45%, while the income tax rates in the United States range from 10% to 37%[9][10].

Cost of Living Comparison: In South Africa, the cost of living is 53.5% lower than in the United States. This means that, on average, goods and services are cheaper in South Africa compared to the United States.

Tax Comparison: Additionally, the analyst in South Africa generally pays less in taxes compared to the analyst in the United States. South Africans will have real wealth due to a lower cost of living with a lower Tax liability given their lower wages but getting more from a buck spent.

---

[8] Data Analyst Salary in South Africa in 2023 | PayScale

[9] Average Salary For Data Analyst In South Africa - 2023/2024 (safacts.co.za) - The average data analyst salary in South Africa is R 746,630 per year or R 383 per hour. Entry-level positions start at R 324 000 per year, while most experienced workers make up to R 7 702 500 per year.

[10] Data analyst salary in South Africa (indeed.com)

Salary Comparison: However, the average monthly net salary (after tax) in South Africa is 72.8% lower than in the United States. In other words, people in South Africa generally earn significantly less than their counterparts in the United States.

Purchasing Power: To put it simply, if an analyst in South Africa earns ZAR 400,000 per year, their purchasing power is roughly equivalent to that of an analyst in the United States earning $50,000 per year. Despite the lower salary in South Africa, the lower cost of living there allows them to have a similar standard of living in terms of what they can afford with their income. This is partially due to the lower tax burden in South Africa.

Therefore, when comparing salaries for analysts across different countries and regions, it is essential to consider the cost of living and taxation as well as other factors, such as currency exchange rates, inflation rates, and quality of life. The above explains why the finance executive had to increase a team member's salary so much after he relocated to New Zealand. In one of his visits, the team member shared how things are financially tighter in the new country and he misses his old life with a five-bedroomed house and helpers as he moved into a small apartment with a small kitchen big enough to allow him to fry one egg at a time. Besides this, we might have to consider double taxing if we retain our South African citizenship. It might be worth it if you are building a work portfolio that focuses on international exposure.

BUILDING A PROJECT PORTFOLIO

Building a strong project portfolio is crucial for aspiring analysts. You can start by working on personal projects or participating in open-source initiatives. I have stumbled upon Fiver.com[11] and similar tools which seem to be doing a great job exposing novice and experienced professionals to clients. It would work in your favour to register on as many platforms as possible for search engine optimisation (SEO). Showcase your ability to solve real-world data problems, highlight Your technical skills, and demonstrate Your understanding of data analysis methodologies. Sharing these projects on platforms like GitHub[12] or creating a personal website can help gain visibility and attract potential employers. The question is "What is needed to obtain a good analyst role?"

HOW TO GET HIRED

To increase your chances of getting hired as an analyst, let us consider the following tips:

- Develop a strong online presence by maintaining an updated LinkedIn profile and engaging in relevant communities,
- Network with professionals in the field through events, meet-ups, and online forums,
- Tailor your resume to highlight your relevant skills and project experience,

[11] Start Selling on Fiverr

[12] GitHub: Let's build from here · GitHub

- Prepare for technical interviews by practising data analysis challenges and familiarising yourself with common interview questions, and
- Showcase your ability to communicate effectively and present your findings clearly and concisely.

Working for a corporation might not be for you. If that is the case, don't stress and there are also ways to showcase talent. Have you thought about the benefits of freelancing?

HOW TO FREELANCE

Freelancing can be a viable option for data analysts especially when being tied to one employer isn't for you. It also is an ideal option for African analysts hoping to score better hourly rates in other well-developed countries, besides international experience. When considering freelancing, it is vital to have the following in place:

- A strong portfolio of projects to showcase your expertise,
- Make sure that you are part of freelancing platforms or marketplaces such as Upwork or Freelancer,
- Having clearly defined rates, and terms of engagement for your services
- Being able to market yourself by leveraging social media platforms and creating a professional website, and
- Networking with potential clients and continuously expanding your professional network.

I hope that the above points will help us avoid some common mistakes we all make. Do you know what are the common mistakes to avoid?

COMMON MISTAKES MADE BY NOVICE DATA ANALYSTS

Novice data analysts often make some common mistakes that can hinder their progress. I use the word novice loosely, but it is really a reflection of bad habits that many of us hold onto because the truth is that these mistakes are not exclusively present in novice analysts. These include:

- Not thoroughly understanding the business context and objectives before diving into data analysis,
- Overlooking data cleaning and pre-processing thus leading to inaccurate insights,
- Focusing solely on technical skills and neglecting the ability to communicate effectively with stakeholders/top management,
- Not documenting or properly organizing code and analysis processes and making it difficult to reproduce or share findings, and
- Failing to continuously update and upskill themselves in the rapidly evolving field of data analysis.

However, there is a shortage of capable hands to handle this demand, and some are turning to artificial intelligence (AI) for assistance. It is important to educate ourselves on the influence of artificial intelligence on employment opportunities, no matter what the field. Do you understand how AI could help you be more productive and provide better opportunities?

IMPACT OF AI ON JOB OPENINGS

While AI has automated certain repetitive tasks, it has also created new opportunities for data analysts. AI and machine learning technologies require data analysts to pre-process and analyse the data for effective implementation. The use of AI is expected to improve the accuracy and effectiveness of data analysis, as well as enhance the quality and impact thereof, which in turn may lead to more job opportunities in the field. Despite concerns about AI becoming self-aware as depicted in science fiction, we are still a long way from that reality. However, AI has progressed faster than predicted due to advancements in processing power and chip technology. Analysts need to consider how they can leverage AI to gain a competitive edge and may need to adapt their skillset accordingly.

AI is aimed at assisting us with repetitive and time-consuming tasks, like data preparation and clean-up. Most of us worry about AI reaching stages of self-awareness stage as depicted in sci-fi movies but the reality is that we are a long way away from that becoming a reality. What is amazing is that AI has progressed faster than forecasted with improved processing power and better computing or processing chips. The question you should be asking at this point is, how can analysts gain a competitive advantage with AI? Let's explore that.

THE IMPACT OF AI AND CHATGPT ON DATA ANALYSIS

While many of us may be worried about how AI will affect and change our daily routines, I was already experiencing the impact of that, as I knew that, sooner or later, a more powerful machine than the well-guarded IBM Watson would eventually impact my job. We had never anticipated it being this quick, especially for those of us working as analysts. It begs the question: While AI offers unprecedented capabilities, are fears of human redundancy well founded? Well, we can't deny that data analysis has become a cornerstone of modern businesses - by extracting valuable insights from raw data, companies can better understand their performance, predict trends, make informed decisions, and create data-driven strategies.

So, the answer is, contrary to those concerns, AI could be the catalyst that not only enhances the role of most analysts but also increases their demand. This is especially true for those capable of synergizing their skill sets with these transformative technologies. With the rise of AI and advanced language models like ChatGPT, the landscape of data analysis is rapidly evolving. But far from making data analysts obsolete, these technologies will likely make their roles even more crucial. AI and machine learning technologies are indisputably transforming the professional landscape, with data analysis roles being one of the fields most impacted. We can see by now how there is an increasing need for future-ready analysts – the ones embracing toolsets that provide better information to top management. The question you could be asking is “For how long will the demand for analysts be?”

A NEED FOR MORE ANALYSTS

The analysis process typically involves several steps: understanding the business context, applying intuition, testing hypotheses, interpreting results, crafting a compelling story, communicating insights, and guiding decision-making. Let’s explore how AI and language models could impact each of these aspects and why data analysts will continue to play a key role.

Business Understanding: This involves understanding the problem at hand and the nature of the data to be analysed. While AI can ingest and process vast amounts of data quickly, the human perspective is essential in identifying the right problems to solve, formulating relevant questions, and determining the type of data needed for analysis. Analysts with a deep understanding of business domains can provide this context, which AI tools currently cannot.

Intuition: Intuition, often honed by years of experience, plays a crucial role in analysis. While AI can detect patterns and correlations in large datasets, it cannot apply intuition in the same way humans can. This ability to hypothesize, anticipate outcomes, or infer underlying issues based on limited data remains a uniquely human capability that supplements the analytical power of AI.

Testing: AI can expedite the testing process by automating repetitive tasks and applying complex algorithms swiftly. However, human oversight is necessary to ensure the appropriateness of tests conducted, verify the accuracy of results, and account for potential bias or error in AI algorithms.

Interpretation: Although AI can process data and provide outputs based on pre-defined criteria, interpreting these results in a meaningful way requires human intervention. Data analysts play a critical role in evaluating AI-generated insights in the context of the business, industry, and broader economic trends.

Storytelling: Translating dry numbers into a compelling narrative that resonates with non-technical audiences is an art. ChatGPT and similar models can help to generate descriptive narratives from data, but crafting an insightful, engaging story that captures the bigger picture and drives action, requires a human touch. Especially a touch of a human analyst with years of hands-on experience.

Communication: AI tools can present findings in a structured and coherent manner, but effective communication requires empathy, persuasion, and the ability to respond to queries in real-time—capabilities that remain distinctly human. Most analysts not only communicate raw findings but also tailor their messages based on the audience's knowledge and perspectives.

Decision-making: AI can provide valuable insights and predictions to inform decision-making, but it cannot make those decisions itself. Analysts leverage their understanding of business needs and constraints to guide data-driven decision-making, ensuring that AI-generated insights align with business strategies and goals.

The above has provided us with a sense of comfort that human analysts are to be better than automated reports. Does this completely answer the question about "AI being for analysts or against analysts?"

AI IS NOT A THREAT BUT A FRIEND

The advent of AI and advanced language models like ChatGPT is not a threat but an opportunity for analysts. As these tools evolve, they will handle more routine tasks, freeing up analysts to focus on high-value tasks that require human intuition, business knowledge, and communication skills. In other words, AI and language models will augment rather than replace human analysts, making them even more critical to business success. Rather than rendering data analysts obsolete, these tools have amplified their capabilities, allowing them to process vast datasets more rapidly and accurately. I know that the advent of AI and its various tools has had a profound impact on data analysis, but not in the way many of us might assume.

KEY TAKEAWAYS

In this chapter we explored the growing demand for data analysts in various industries, emphasizing the need for a comprehensive guide to becoming a skilled data analyst in the future; we covered essential aspects such as the expected demand, necessary skills, tools, academic background, salaries, building a project portfolio, getting hired, freelancing, and common mistakes made by novice data analysts. Furthermore, we addressed the impact of AI, especially ChatGPT, on the field of data analysis, highlighting the positive potential for data analysts rather than rendering them obsolete.

Below is a synopsis of things that are crucial to remember:

1. **Growing Demand for Analysts:** The demand for skilled analysts is expected to remain high in the future as organisations increasingly value data-driven decision-making across industries such as finance, healthcare, e-commerce, marketing, and technology.

2. **Essential Skills:** Successful data analysts should possess a combination of technical and practical skills, including proficiency in programming languages like Python and R, a solid understanding of statistical concepts and data visualization techniques, expertise in SQL and database management, knowledge of machine learning algorithms, and excellent problem-solving abilities.

3. Commonly Used Tools: Data analysts rely on various tools, such as Python, R, SQL, Tableau, and Excel, to efficiently perform their tasks. Familiarity with these tools is essential for success in the field.

4. Academic Background: While there is no strict academic path, a background in mathematics, statistics, computer science, economics, or engineering can provide a solid foundation for aspiring data analysts. Pursuing relevant certifications or data analysis boot camps can also enhance employability.

5. Salaries: Analyst salaries vary based on experience, qualifications, and location. African analysts may find higher earning potential in international markets through freelancing and taking advantage of outsourcing opportunities.

6. Building a Project Portfolio: Aspiring data analysts should focus on building a strong project portfolio by working on personal projects and participating in open-source initiatives. Showcasing expertise on platforms like GitHub can attract potential employers.

7. Getting Hired: Increasing the chances of getting hired involves maintaining an updated LinkedIn profile, networking with professionals in the field, tailoring resumes to highlight relevant skills and project experience, and preparing for technical interviews.

8. Freelancing: Freelancing can be a viable option for data analysts, especially when seeking higher hourly rates in international markets. Building a strong portfolio, joining freelancing platforms, and marketing oneself effectively is key to freelancing success.

9. Common Mistakes: Novice data analysts should avoid common mistakes such as overlooking data cleaning and pre-processing, neglecting communication skills, and failing to continuously update their skill set.

10. The Impact of AI and ChatGPT on Data Analysis: AI, including ChatGPT, has transformed data analysis but is not in the way of making data analysts obsolete. Instead, AI augments their roles by handling routine tasks, allowing analysts to focus on higher-value functions like interpretation, communication, and decision-making.

11. A Bright Future for Data Analysts: Analysts who embrace AI tools and work synergistically with them will remain relevant and in demand. Human intuition, business understanding, and communication skills will continue to be valuable aspects in an AI-driven world.

Overall, the chapter provides valuable insights into the dynamic field of data analysis, offering guidance for aspiring analysts to navigate the impact of AI and seize opportunities for a successful career in 2023 and beyond.

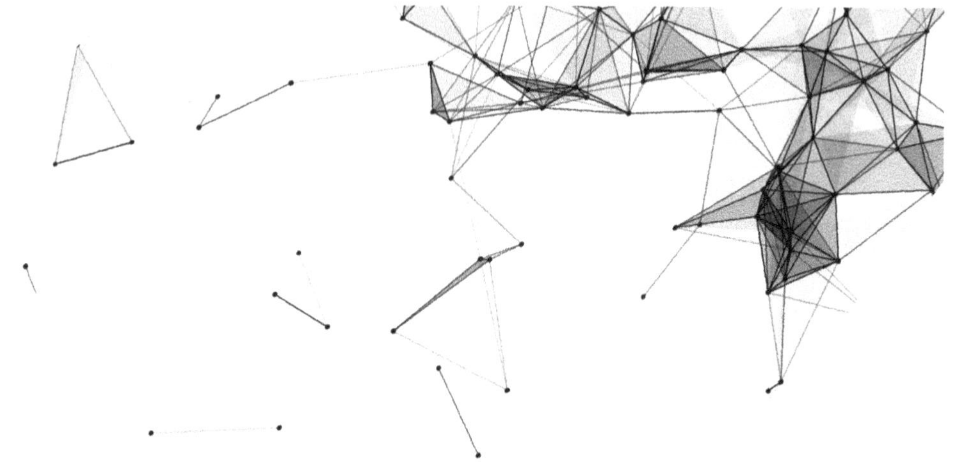

chapter 2

A PATHWAY TO BECOMING AN ANALYST - NURTURING YOUR PATH TO EXCELLENCE

After reading numerous questions about how one could start being an analyst nowadays, I began reflecting on how best to answer this: "How to become an analyst?" The world of analysis offers many exciting career opportunities for individuals with a knack for problem-solving, critical thinking, and data interpretation. If you are considering embarking on a career as an analyst, there are several distinct pathways you can explore. In this chapter, I will discuss five options to help you kick-start your journey as an analyst. Let's get straight into it:

- Being an Analyst through Education,
- Job Internship or Job Secondment,
- Attending Masterclasses,
- Using Company Learning and Development Resources, and
- Joining Analyst Communities.

By understanding these diverse routes, you can make an informed decision on the most suitable path for your aspirations.

BEING AN ANALYST THROUGH EDUCATION

Education plays a vital role in developing the foundational skills and knowledge necessary for a successful career in analysis. Pursuing a relevant degree such as statistics, mathematics, economics, or business analytics provides a strong academic foundation. These programs typically offer data analysis, statistical modelling, and data visualization coursework, equipping you with the necessary technical skills. I understood this as early as when I left high school. My mother cemented the idea that all is possible through education and thus this has become my preferred path to anything career-related.

In addition to formal education, you can also expand your knowledge by attending workshops, seminars, or online courses that focus on specific analytical tools or techniques. I have found time during work to enrol in quick LinkedIn[13] training sessions to gain an overview of a concept. Platforms like Coursera[14],

---

[13] LinkedIn Learning: Online Courses for Creative, Technology, Business Skills

[14] Coursera Plus | Unlimited Access to 7,000+ Online Courses

Udemy[15], and edX[16] offer various data analysis courses taught by industry professionals, allowing you to improve your skills and stay up-to-date with the latest trends. It's important to pursue what you love and not just what others recommend. Remember, you will face the exams/assessments alone. If you were not admitted to further studies or do not have a stable internet connection for online courses, you may consider looking for internships.

JOB INTERNSHIP OR JOB SECONDMENT

There have been a lot of programmes created here in South Africa. This was to address the high unemployment rate among the youth, as compared to other countries. These internships are designed as an excellent way to gain practical experience in analysis through job internships or job secondments. Internships provide valuable exposure to real-world scenarios, enabling you to apply your theoretical knowledge in a professional setting. “Move-up” programmes like “YES” (Youth Employment Service's)[17] could be a great way for novice analysts to get a foot in the door. Current analysts recommend that you seek internships at organisations that emphasize data-driven decision-making, as this will allow you to work alongside experienced analysts and learn from their expertise.

Alternatively, if you are already employed in a different role within an organisation, explore the possibility of a job secondment. A

---

[15] Online Courses - Learn Anything, On Your Schedule | Udemy

[16] Build new skills. Advance your career. | edX

[17] The Youth Employment Service (YES) - a South African business-driven initiative aimed at addressing the issue of youth unemployment in the country. YES was launched in 2018 and operates as a partnership between government, business, and labour. Its primary goal is to provide work experience and job opportunities to unemployed youth in South Africa.

secondment offers you the chance to temporarily work within an analytical team or department, allowing you to acquire hands-on experience while still benefiting from the security of your existing job. There is a way to combine both the internship and job secondment to your advantage. You could start with the "move up" programme and then ask to shadow someone in the data team. Some tasks like copying and pasting graphs might be yours and before you know it you are a team administrator or business office manager. You might even attend some masterclasses being offered by team members during your secondment tenure.

ATTENDING MASTERCLASSES

Masterclasses, workshops, and industry conferences provide excellent opportunities to learn from leading analysts and industry experts. Thanks to the Covid-19 pandemic, I found that more sessions are free of charge and held online. These events often focus on specific analytical domains, such as marketing analytics, financial analysis, or data science. By attending masterclasses, you can gain insights into advanced analytical techniques, discover practical case studies, and network with professionals in the field. This will give you the opportunity to decide if the area tickles your fancy before you commit.

South Africa hosts several conferences and events related to various types of analysts, including data analysts, financial analysts, business analysts, and more. These conferences provide opportunities for analysts to network, learn about the latest industry trends, and share insights. I would advise also to look for renowned international conferences like the Analytics Summit,

Strata Data Conference, or Predictive Analytics World, where you can interact with thought leaders and engage in discussions that can broaden your understanding of analysis.

Business Analysis Summit: This is the official conference of the South African chapter of IIBA, the International Institute of Business Analysis. It is a platform for business analysts and stakeholders to share knowledge, network, and learn from experts. The theme for the 2023 summit is "Elevate. Empower. Excel: Inspiring the Future of Business Analysis". It was held in Cape Town from October 30 to November 1, 2023[18].

IITPSA Business Analysts Summit: Organized by the Institute of Information Technology Professionals South Africa (IITPSA)[19], this event is aimed at business analysts and covers various aspects of business analysis, including methodologies, tools, and best practices.

Data Analysis Conferences: These are conferences that focus on various aspects of data analysis, such as data science, machine learning, artificial intelligence, big data, and more. They are aimed at researchers, practitioners, and students who want to explore the latest trends and innovations in data analysis. Some examples of data analysis conferences in South Africa are:

1. The International Conference on Data Science and Applications (DSA 2023), which was being held in Johannesburg from March 13 to 15, 2023.
2. The International Conference on Machine Learning and Data Mining (MLDM 2023), was be held in Cape Town from July 17 to 21, 2023.
3. The International Conference on Artificial Intelligence and Big Data (AIBD 2023), was be held in Durban from September 11 to 13, 2023.

---

[18] Business Analysis Summit | Business Analysis Summit Southern Africa (basummit.co.za)

[19] Upcoming Events - IITPSA

Risk and Assurance Insights Conference: This conference focuses on risk management, governance, and assurance. While not exclusively for analysts, it often includes sessions and discussions relevant to risk analysts and auditors[20].

Finite-State Methods and Natural Language Processing (FSMNLP): This is a conference that covers topics related to finite-state methods and their applications in natural language processing, such as morphology, syntax, semantics, speech recognition, text generation, and more. It is a forum for researchers and practitioners to exchange ideas and results on this field. The fifteenth FSMNLP 2023 was be held in Stellenbosch from August 28 to 30, 2023[21]

ITWeb Business Intelligence Summit: This conference focuses on business intelligence, data analytics, and related topics[22]. It typically features expert speakers, workshops, and discussions on the latest developments in business analytics.

CFA Society South Africa Conference: This event is organized by the CFA Society South Africa[23] and is primarily for financial analysts and investment professionals. It covers topics related to investment management, finance, and economics.

DataCon South Africa: This conference focuses on data analytics, big data, and data science. It brings together data professionals, including data analysts, data scientists, and data engineers, to explore the latest trends and technologies in the field[24].

---

[20] Deloitte Africa Risk Conference 2021 | Event

[21] FSMNLP 2023 in Stellenbosch

[22] ITWeb Business Intelligence Summit 2023

[23] Upcoming Events - CFA Society South Africa

[24] DataCon Africa 2023 - Home (coriniumintelligence.com)

USING COMPANY LEARNING AND DEVELOPMENT RESOURCES

Many organisations offer learning and development resources to help their employees build new skills and enhance their competencies. If yours does the same, you can take advantage of these resources by enrolling in internal training programs, accessing online learning platforms provided by your company, or participating in mentorship programs. Seek guidance from senior analysts within your organisation who can offer valuable insights and mentorship to accelerate your growth as an analyst. My organisation had boot camps designed with analysts in mind. These boot camp communities do more to advance analysts, even tailor-making training materials.

JOINING ANALYST COMMUNITIES

Joining analyst communities and professional networks can provide immense value in terms of knowledge-sharing and networking opportunities. Platforms like LinkedIn and Reddit have numerous communities dedicated to data analysis, where professionals share their experiences, discuss emerging trends, and offer advice. Engaging in these communities can help you stay informed about the latest advancements, connect with like-minded individuals, and seek guidance from experienced analysts. I know this is popular among male analysts while things might be slightly different for mid-career female analysts.

ANALYST JOB SEARCH ADVICE FOR WOMEN

Looking for a new job can be both thrilling and difficult, particularly for women in their mid-career years between the ages of 25 and 45. I have read numerous accounts of how women prioritize security over their happiness and potential. As someone who was raised by a single mother, I can relate to this mentality. My parents divorced when I was only ten years old, and my mother raised me without ever remarrying. My sisters stepped in to fill the void left by my absent father. Sometimes, what you have to do to support your family can conflict with your career aspirations.

My siblings' selfless sacrifices and dedication to helping my brothers and me succeed are truly admirable. They put their job search on hold to ensure our survival, but you do not have to do the same. Especially not this year. I want to remind you that, with the right mindset and strategies, you can stand out from the crowd and unlock incredible opportunities. Let us explore empowering advice that can help female analysts confidently navigate the job market and achieve their career objectives.

Embrace Your Unique Qualities as Female Analyst

Stop beating yourself up for not having a degree or any specific qualification that you think is holding you back. Yes, this is coming from a guy with seven qualifications and still counting. I am not saying this to look down on you at all. Instead, let me remind you to shift your mindset and focus on the valuable skills, experiences, and strengths you possess. Recognise that every individual brings a unique set of abilities to the table, and it's crucial to highlight what you have to offer. Degrees aren't the start or end of the world. By embracing your unique qualities, you will gain the confidence to showcase your worth to potential employers and make a lasting impression. This is called personal branding or Personovation[25] as Timothy Maurice Webster puts it.

Build Your Personal Brand

To stand out from the competition, it's essential to build a strong personal brand. Some of us see this as water and oil. This is where personal innovation becomes important, especially as an analyst. You do this by identifying your unique value proposition—the qualities and expertise that make you different from others. Highlight your achievements, skills, and passions that align with your desired industry or job role. Leverage social media platforms, professional networking events, and online communities to share your knowledge, insights, and experiences. By establishing yourself as an authority in your field, you will become a sought-after professional, joining the 1% who stand out from the rest. This is where ladies like Nobesuthu Mahlangu, Tshwanelo Fokazi, and other social media mentors could assist you in building something strong. Doing so will allow you to share your achievements while you are still polishing your confidence for face-to-face engagements.

[25] Personovation is a journey of personal innovation that involves re-inventing your personal brand to live a more fulfilled life.

Boldly Share Your Achievements

One of the keys to success in the job market is confidently showcasing your accomplishments. It's time to overcome the fear of "bragging" about yourself. Remember, the job market is highly competitive, and if you don't take the opportunity to pitch yourself, someone else will beat you to the punch, and pitch themselves in your stead. Embrace the art of self-promotion and become fluent in articulating your achievements, skills, and unique selling points. Top management won't know about your potential if you are not selling yourself. Your team leader and other managers are too occupied selling themselves hence no one is your advocate. 'Hetty the Entrepreneur' encourages us not only to continue bragging, but also to monetise our achievements.

Share your success stories during interviews, on your resume, and through networking channels. By effectively communicating your value, you position yourself as a winning candidate. Remember that the internet is a great equaliser. You would have never heard my voice if it wasn't for the internet and the resources that allowed me to self-publish this book. Do the work in self-promotion and show how others can benefit from being associated with your brand.

Go the Extra Mile

Differentiate yourself by going above and beyond what others typically do. Stand out by sending customized thank you videos to everyone you interview with. This is not just cooking but doing the culinary award plating – icing on the top! This gesture demonstrates your genuine interest, gratitude, and attention to detail. By taking this extra step, you will exemplify your professionalism, enthusiasm, and dedication to the position. Such personalized actions make you a memorable candidate and showcase your commitment to excellence, setting you apart from the majority. At this point, you might be asking yourself "How do you become an excellent analyst?"

NURTURING YOUR PATH TO EXCELLENCE

We have all seen people in great careers, that we aspire to occupy, what made it worse is when they left those positions, in pursuit of something they love. Why would they do this? Is there something they know that the rest of us don't? Well, in the quest for personal and professional development, intentional growth emerges as a guiding light, illuminating the path to success. This happens with purposeful actions and steadfast determination. While accidental growth may offer fleeting comfort, intentional growth empowers individuals to take charge of their journey, fostering resilience, adaptability, and long-lasting achievement. Individuals with intentional growth have the above characteristics. They choose rather to: insist on starting today, take complete responsibility to grow, often learn before mistakes, rely on hard work, persevere long and hard, fight for good habits, follow through, take risks, think like a learner, rely on character, and they never stop learning.

Insisting on Starting Today

Intentional growth begins with the firm resolve to start today, dismissing the allure of procrastination. Working with these people might seem like they are pushy. This proactive approach ensures that every moment counts, propelling them toward their goals without delay. By capitalizing on the present, intentional growth harnesses time as a valuable ally, paving the way for gradual, consistent progress.

I once saw a post that read, “Start Now, Start Where You Are, Start with Fear, Start With Pain, Start With Doubt, Start With What You Have...Start and Don’t Stop”. This could be our ticket out of procrastination, and we should own it.

Takes Complete Responsibility to Grow

In the realm of intentional growth, individuals wholeheartedly embrace the responsibility to craft their own destinies. They recognize that their growth is their own creation, driven by their choices and actions. This accountability fuels a sense of ownership, enabling them to steer their lives toward their desired outcomes resulting in abundant learning.

Often Learns Before Mistakes

While accidental growth often occurs when we learn from mistakes rather than seeking continuous improvement, intentional growth emphasizes learning from others and seeking knowledge proactively, even before mistakes are made. This approach will enable us to pre-emptively equip ourselves with the skills and insights required to navigate challenges effectively. By adopting a continuous learning mindset, we enhance our competence and foresight. I know that doing this is harder than learning from mistakes.

Relies on Hard Work

Unlike accidental growth, which relies on luck, intentional growth places its trust in diligent effort and hard work. It acknowledges that true success is the fruit of consistent labour, commitment, and dedication. By dedicating ourselves to relentless improvement, we cultivate a strong work ethic that fuels our journey to excellence.

Perseveres Long and Hard

Intentional growth champions perseverance, understanding that progress often involves enduring adversity. It refuses to succumb to setbacks and obstacles, choosing instead to persist with resilience and unwavering determination. This resilience transforms challenges into opportunities for growth. I have seen how the adoption of this mindset can change everything.

Fighting for Good Habits

One of the cornerstones of intentional growth is the commitment to cultivating good habits. The Book, "Atomic Habits" by James Clear and others like it, show how easily we could slip into bad habits. But people focused on intentional growth, actively work to replace detrimental behaviours with positive routines that propel them forward. I still battle with the admin of tracking my habits but I hope you have better luck in this. This conscientious effort results in a strong foundation for continuous improvement.

Follows Through

Intentional growth hinges on following through with commitments and goals. Unlike accidental growth, which lacks a strategic plan, intentional growth involves a structured approach to completing tasks and fulfilling promises. This consistency builds trust and demonstrates reliability.

Takes Risks

Intentional growth encourages stepping out of comfort zones and taking calculated risks. These risks are seen as opportunities for expansion and exploration, driving individuals to confront new challenges and discover untapped potential. Such risks contribute to personal development and resilience.

Thinks Like a Learner

I know we all think we are learners especially when we have completed university. But intentional growth focuses on now and not your past. It cultivates a learner's mindset, embracing every experience as an opportunity to gain insights and knowledge. It is like what life was like when you were still keen to explore new things. This openness to learning allows individuals to continuously evolve, adapting to changing circumstances and emerging stronger.

Never Stops Learning

A hallmark of intentional growth is the commitment to lifelong learning. This is because we should recognise that personal mastery is a perpetual pursuit, transcending formal education. It is for this reason that I love writing about topics that focus on personal mastery. I believe personal mastery is a forever education that ends when we die. This thirst for knowledge ensures that individuals remain adaptable, relevant, and ahead of the curve.

Relies on Character

Talent is not all that is required in life. Central to intentional growth is the development of strong character. Unlike relying on our talents, character involves cultivating qualities such as integrity, discipline, and empathy. These attributes serve as a moral compass, guiding individuals on their journey while fostering trust and respect from peers and colleagues.

ADVANTAGES AND DISADVANTAGES OF INTENTIONAL GROWTH

We can see the benefit of intentional growth, especially for analysts. Some advantages to highlight include fostering proactive and purposeful development, building a strong foundation of skills and knowledge, increasing adaptability and resilience, cultivating a strong work ethic and commitment, enhancing personal accountability and ownership, and positioning yourself for sustained success. The disadvantages of intentional growth could include demanding sustained effort and perseverance, stepping out of comfort zones which often leads to places of discomfort, leading to higher expectations and responsibilities, and balancing multiple growth pursuits that might be challenging.

Intentional growth stands in stark contrast to accidental growth, which hinges on luck, procrastination, and reactive learning from mistakes. Unlike accidental growth, intentional growth thrives on conscious effort, proactive planning, and a perpetual hunger for self-improvement. While accidental growth may offer fleeting advantages, it ultimately falls short of fostering lasting progress and resilience. Intentional growth, with its focus on perseverance, character development, and continuous learning, offers a roadmap to personal mastery and enduring success. In a world of opportunities, embracing intentional growth is the key to unlocking one's true potential and realizing a fulfilled purpose-driven life.

KEY TAKEAWAYS

Just to recap- in this chapter we discussed five distinct pathways to kick-start a career as an analyst, guiding education, job internships or secondments, attending masterclasses, utilizing company learning resources, and joining analyst communities - I cannot overemphasize the value of education (paid or free online), practical experience, and networking in becoming a successful data analyst - Additionally, this chapter offers empowering advice for women in the job market, encouraging them to embrace their unique qualities, build a strong personal brand, confidently share achievements, and go the extra mile to stand out as exceptional candidates.

The following are the points that are crucial to remember:

1. **Pathways to Becoming an Analyst:** Aspiring analysts can explore different routes, such as pursuing a relevant education, gaining practical experience through job internships or secondments, attending masterclasses and industry conferences, accessing company learning resources, and joining analyst communities to network and stay informed.

2. **Education and Skill Development:** A relevant degree in statistics, mathematics, economics, or business analytics provides a strong academic foundation. Additionally, attending workshops, seminars, or online courses can help

improve technical skills and stay updated with industry trends.

3. **Practical Experience:** Job internships and secondments offer valuable exposure to real-world scenarios and provide opportunities to work alongside experienced analysts, accelerating skill development.

4. **Industry Events and Networking:** Attending masterclasses, workshops, and conferences allows analysts to learn from leading experts and network with professionals in the field, expanding their knowledge and career opportunities.

5. **Utilizing Company Resources:** Taking advantage of learning and development resources provided by employers, enrolling in internal training programs, and seeking mentorship from senior analysts can enhance growth as an analyst.

6. **Empowering Women in the Job Market:** Women can confidently navigate the job market by embracing their unique qualities, building a strong personal brand, confidently sharing achievements, and going the extra mile to stand out from competitors.

7. **Overcoming Limiting Beliefs:** Women especially should focus on their strengths and accomplishments, shifting their mindset to recognize their value and worth in the job market.

8. **Building a Personal Brand:** Creating a personal brand by highlighting achievements, skills, and passions aligning with the desired industry or job role can set candidates apart from others.

9. **Effective Self-Promotion:** Confidently articulating achievements and unique selling points during interviews, on resumes, and through networking channels enhances candidates' chances of success.

10. **Demonstrating Commitment:** Differentiating oneself by going above and beyond typical job-search practices, such as sending personalized thank-you videos, showcasing dedication and professionalism, and making candidates more memorable and attractive to potential employers.

11. **Seizing Opportunities:** By leveraging strengths, embracing self-belief, and adopting effective job search strategies, women can unlock incredible opportunities and achieve their career objectives.

Overall, the chapter provides aspiring data analysts with valuable insights into various pathways for entering the field and empowers women to confidently navigate the job market, showcasing their unique skills and strengths to stand out as exceptional candidates.

chapter 3

ROADMAP TO BECOMING A PROFICIENT ANALYST

The need for analysis has grown so much over the years. I started my data analysis career running away from managing debits and credits as an assistant financial officer. Over time the world at large seemed to realise that there isn't enough attention given to analyse all the data we have accumulated. Added to that, smartphones and other portable devices made doing everything easier to the point that we all started using them, for just about everything. In so doing, we created more platforms to collect even more data. The need for a better and faster way to analyse data created a need for standalone data analysts, who specialised specifically in this field. Thus a new career was born.

Those who began working in data analysis and visualization during the 2010s remember being drawn to the field out of necessity. Formal training was not required; instead, it was important to select hardworking individuals who were proficient in using data manipulation applications and software. We were given different titles, such as Business Analyst, Data Analyst, and in my case, 'Sales Operations Reporting Manager'. Despite our different titles, we were all responsible for managing data at various levels.

Recently, I discovered that the data field has attracted many people. Everyone is seeking the magic formula to become a data analyst, but it is important to note that theory alone will not make someone an analyst, and neither are the steps that I took to establish myself. At the time, there was a need and high demand, so even those with mediocre analytical skills could have a good career. But today things are different. Universities have been called upon to assist with formal training, thus the never-ending list of courses with 'data' and 'analytics' variations in the title. I did a course in 'big data analytics'; I have never needed to analyse big data.

The big data courses were the ones I was particularly interested in until I came across a five-page document created to assist anyone who wants to be a data scientist[26][27]. The document is well-

[26] Data Science Roadmap 2023: Learn To Become a Data Scientist (skillslane.com) - In this roadmap for data science learning, you can understand different verticals for data science and the areas you need to focus on if you are getting started with data science.

[27] https://www.linkedin.com/posts/nollie-maoto-108a6025_the-data-scientist-roadmap-activity-7042003305731866625-bhU1?utm_source=share&utm_medium=member_desktop - A very useful Data Scientist Roadmap for anyone new to the data science field created by The Ravit Show.

written in a large font, ensuring that everyone can follow the process. However, I soon realised that what was written on this document is like what is said on social media, but despite that, there is definitely a need for this type of document as we are not all in the same social media circles. There are typically ten steps highlighted for one to follow if you are thinking of a data science career namely:

1. Learning mathematical (Math) fundamental concepts
2. Learning how to program computer systems
3. Data wrangling and visualisation
4. Statistics and probability concepts
5. Understanding of databases
6. Machine learning
7. Practising what you are learning
8. Big data Concepts
9. Learning advanced concepts
10. Implementation – getting analyst job/project

MATH FUNDAMENTALS

It is always encouraged that each school graduate should have math basics. If you are one of those who opted out of maths and science in high school, don't be distressed. Various resources could assist you with understanding concepts of linear algebra, calculus, optimisation, and functions. Don't worry about having a doctorate equivalent in any of the concepts. Remember that the software will do the work. You just must learn the basic math concepts and you will be good as a computer programmer. You might ask "How does math concepts link with computer programming?"

LEARN PROGRAMMING

Learning math concepts helped me translate them into computer language, and the same is true for many programmers. This is the equivalent of using a calculator instead of scribing the entire math solution on paper. Calculators are handy especially when I don't have scribbling tools or can't keep up the sum in my head. Learning how to program is equivalent to me learning how to compute complex math problems using a calculator. Knowing how the computer needs to be punched (inputted) improved my output tenfold. I decided to enrol on an IT management degree at university and I learned VBA and SQL programming languages. I then took big data in my post-graduate degree. There are options for self-study now or even guided online tutorials to assist with pace. Others online suggest that Python and Computer Science (CS) fundamentals could yield better results. I have seen that there are many online resources to help us learn CS and other data-related fields[28]. Programming makes it easier to wrestle data and visualise it appropriately.

[28] Explore Computer Programming Courses and Programs | edX - Discover various computer programming courses and programs to enhance your coding skills for front-end and back-end web development, machine learning, iOS and Android app development, and other related fields. You can take these classes online through edX to learn how to code effectively.

DATA WRANGLING AND VISUALISATION

Learning how to code, assists with data wrangling. Data wrangling techniques include data collection, cleaning the data, and data exploration. This step is important in case you are appointed to the project as a data scientist and there are no data engineers or data analysts to assist with data wrangling. Data visualisation will also assist in data storytelling. You must remember that data storytelling is about what happened to that data along the path, to showing the end result. This will include how data was received, cleaned, and truncated to remove duplicates and all other steps taken before analysis could commence. Being able to visualise this would help keep the audience engaged- especially keeping non-technical audiences in top management (Exco/Manco) who understand the importance of quantitative analysis and rather want a simple-to-read report. We might still have a fear of math and ask "Whether statistics and probability hard to understand?"

STATISTICS AND PROBABILITY

Another way to keep an audience engaged is by showing statistics and probabilities. You will be relieved to know that statistics is not hard to understand at all. Beside, it is the best way to learn how to conduct descriptive statistics. I do descriptive statistics just to let my audience know the min, max, mean, and mode. Khan Academy explains mean, median, and mode as being different measures of center in a numerical data set. They each try to summarize a dataset with a single number to represent a "typical" data point from the dataset[29].

There are other statistical concepts that we learned in the first year of my finance degree at university that could be extremely useful. This includes inferential, associative, and differential[30]. Probability is extremely important. I learned this the hard way when I was writing my master's dissertation (thesis). Conditional probability and Bayes Theorem[31] could do wonders too. I was lucky my supervisor was there to guide me to use the correct statistical algorithms using SPSS and SAS. At least I knew enough about data and storage (databases) although I was new to these software tools.

UNDERSTANDING DATABASES

My understanding of databases started in 2006. I used Microsoft Access when I had an assignment for the Business Information Systems (BIS) module. This module was needed as part of my BCom Finance qualification. Attending university allowed me the opportunity to learn complementary skills to finance. Back then I saw no point in learning databases. It was when I started working that I saw the power of Microsoft SQL Server Management. I had a support group to assist me with my learning, and I learnt that storing data in databases is better than using text files. This is the reason why most companies are using relational databases instead files. Learning this will add value to the company and thus

[29] Mean, median, and mode review (article) | Khan Academy

[30] 4. Probability, Inferential Statistics, and Hypothesis Testing – Beginner Statistics for Psychology (bccampus.ca)

[31] Bayes' Theorem and Conditional Probability | Brilliant Math & Science Wiki

your employment. In 2009 I discovered a website that helped me unpack Structured Query Language (SQL) as this was in only two chapters of a software engineering book[32]. That website is still running today[33]. If I were to start all over again, I would learn about converting files to databases.

LEARN MACHINE LEARNING

My first encounter with Machine Learning (ML) was daunting. I enrolled for the optimisation elective module for my post-graduate in Informatics. I came from work, all formal, and walked into a class full of people wearing sweats, only to encounter a screen that seemed like a Nokia snake game. I was told that was my assignment for the semester. I had to successfully program something that would learn not to crush on itself. There are lots of terminologies being used in class. These terminologies are important for effective communication. They speak of supervised learning, unsupervised learning, time series, or dimensionality reduction (clustering) techniques. Some are close to big data thus learning Hadoop and ML will be beneficial. This is the same reason why I chose both Big Data and Optimisation elective modules.

I was terrified when I was doing my honours (post-graduate) degree in Informatics. I sometimes wanted to drop both Big Data

---

[32] Software Engineering by Ian Sommerville, Edition 9, Pearson Education, 2011, ISBN0133001490, 9780133001495

[33] SQL Tutorial (w3schools.com) - Learn how to store, manipulate, and retrieve data in databases using SQL - a widely accepted standard language. This tutorial covers the usage of SQL in various database systems including MySQL, SQL Server, MS Access, Oracle, Sybase, Informix, Postgres, and others.

and Optimisation modules because getting a passing mark was more important that learning difficult concepts. I dropped Optimisation but am now finding it difficult to learn ML unsupervised. Find your rhythm and get help to learn as much as possible, irrespective of how much you want to quit, and rather watch YouTube videos about money and wealth. It is important to find a tribe of friends who also want to achieve a career in Data Analytics/Science. This way you will be helping each other. Overall, practising and learning from our mistakes is the best way to test ourselves.

FINDING WAYS TO PRACTISE

I have received a lot of advice on how I could get data online and practice what I have learned. The truth is that I battled to do this self-paced practice. I knew that I had to have good hands-on experience otherwise I would forget all that I had learned. The online data download route wasn't for me. The option that most don't talk about is taking bold moves at work- finding big and hairy data projects and volunteering to solve them for the team. It's better if the executive becomes your sponsor in that project. Having the pressure to deliver was better for me compared to self-paced experimentations. It might be hard to have access to business executives like I did. Maybe finding data hackathons could also do the same trick for you as an aspiring data analyst.

LEARNING BIG DATA

Based on web search results, big data analytics is the use of advanced methods and tools to collect, process, and analyse large and diverse data sets from various sources. Big data analytics can help organisations discover patterns, trends, and insights that can improve decision-making, performance, and profitability. Some examples of big data sources are the web, mobile, social media, sensors, transactions, and more. I got introduced to this as a module at university. I first found it daunting to be able to work on Hadoop using software tools that aren't Microsoft SQL Server Management Studio. It was with some practice that I realised the variations between working on manageable (small) databases using local or server storage compared to those big or ambiguous enough that they are being stored in Hadoop. The best part is that I haven't had a project at work that required me to work on Hadoop yet.

LEARNING ADVANCED CONCEPTS

My best self-advice has been to always stay hungry for personal development. It is because I have never been content with what I have nor have I thought something is beyond me. This attitude has allowed me the ability to learn things that are outside of my reach. It was back in 2016 when I proposed to replace financial officers with Power BI. I had no advanced knowledge of Power BI at the time. Fast forward to 2022, everyone in the department was required to be an intermediate user of Power BI.

This decision helped cover the productivity impact because of natural attrition. That was not the end for me and I rather wanted to pursue data science. In so doing, I enrolled on Business Intelligence & Data Analysis training (BIDA) given by the

Corporate Finance Institute (CFI)[34]. This training filled in a lot of gaps and misconceptions I had about data science, data analysis, and business intelligence. The question might be weather "Is it easier today to get a job as an analyst with knowledge of advanced concepts?".

GETTING AN ANALYST JOB (PROJECT/EMPLOYMENT)

Getting a data job is easier today than it was back in 2010 in my opinion. This is because back then employers didn't fully understand what they wanted analysts to solve for them but they knew something wasn't right. Now we have well-informed business leaders who understand the value of data analytics. Your work will be easier the minute a business analyst hands you a business case and you realise that all is well laid out. It will be like you are being paid for nothing. Internships and data boot camps could also be great places to learn. Although I have never experienced either internships or data boot camps. I just went head-on and asked for a job because I had a good value proposition. There are online resources where you can list your expertise and hourly rate for customers to book you. This could be a great training ground, and you will be working with people outside your normal working hours.

---

[34] Become a Certified Business Intelligence & Data Analyst (BIDA) (corporatefinanceinstitute.com) - Looking to launch or enhance your career in data analysis? Look no further than CFI's Business Intelligence & Data Analyst Certification Program. Our courses cover all aspects of BI and data science, from data collection and storage to analysis and visualization, so you can master the most popular tools and programming languages in the field. With real-world case studies and best practices, you'll be ready to perform at a high level in any data role. Earn your certificate in data analytics and business intelligence by enrolling today!

Embarking on a journey to secure an analyst job can be both exhilarating and challenging. I know this because I feel I have attended many interviews both as a candidate and hiring manager. As you transition from a training phase to the real world of professional opportunities, it's essential to keep certain perspectives in mind. Let us not fall into the quick schemes on social media. Hiring managers are also watching the same video you are marking as a game changer. The internet isn't that big after all. In this chapter, let us delve into crucial insights for analysts seeking employment, highlighting the importance of resilience and personal branding. This will be important for you to bounce back after many rejections.

The Best Candidate Can Face Rejection

Imagine a scenario where you've aced the interviews, demonstrated your skills, and aligned perfectly with the job description. Yet, despite your impressive qualifications, you receive the unfortunate news that the position has been filled by someone else. I have been here many times. This reality underscores a fundamental truth: even when you're the best fit on paper, external factors can influence selection processes. We must remember that the job description doesn't show the values the hiring manager is seeking. Your adherence to the job description could fool AI machines but human hiring managers might pick on your tone and choose otherwise. It's a reminder that job selection can be unpredictable, and rejection doesn't diminish your abilities.

Unsuccessful Applications as Divine Direction

The job you didn't land might feel like a missed opportunity. In the grand scheme of things, it might have been a redirection towards something better suited for your growth. Let us use this as a chance to reassess our aspirations, fine-tune our skill set, or explore new avenues. I have fallen many times to defining my role on technical abilities while others saw my ability to run the entire project. Being hired for a technical role would have frustrated me. But I didn't know that was what the panel saw. All I saw was the missed job placement. Let us trust that each rejection might lead us to a more fitting role—one that aligns more closely with our long-term goals.

Rejection is Redirection, not Rejection

Reframing rejection as redirection can help us alleviate the emotional weight of not getting a particular job. Instead of perceiving it as a personal failing, let us now view it as a nudge toward a different path. A path we might have known but feared taking. Sometimes, God (if you are religious) has His own plans, steering you towards opportunities that align more precisely with your strengths and aspirations. Let us focus on the redirection and not dwell on the rejection.

Your Worth is Intrinsic

Remember, your value isn't determined by external opinions or decisions. This is harder to remember when we are faced with a series of rejections. Just because one door is closed doesn't mean our capabilities diminish. We still have those degrees, we still own that suit, and we still know analysis. Our worth is constant and shouldn't be swayed by anyone's inability to fully appreciate our potential. Let us keep faith in our abilities and remain committed to our journey.

Perseverance Pays Off

Believing in ourselves and persisting through challenges are crucial components of achieving success. If the door you've been knocking on remains closed, let us remember that perseverance can lead us to the right door. Let us open a new chapter that embraces setbacks as part of our growth story and let them fuel our determination to succeed.

Crafting Your Personal Brand

In the pursuit of professional advancement, personal branding can play a pivotal role. It's more than just a buzzword; it's a way to communicate your values, vision, and work ethic effectively. Here's how to start building and enhancing your personal brand:

- *Early Start*: Personal branding isn't limited to experienced professionals. Begin cultivating your brand from the onset of your career. It's an evolving process that gains depth as you gain experience.
- *Strengths and Passions*: Reflect on your strengths and passions. Identify what makes you unique and how these qualities can add value to potential employers. A well-defined personal brand stems from self-awareness.

- *Consistency*: Align your actions with your brand. If you tout time management as a strength, for instance, consistently display punctuality and effective scheduling.
- *Validation is Optional*: Your personal brand reflects your true self. It doesn't require validation from others to hold value. Confidence in your brand will resonate with employers and colleagues alike.

Embarking on a journey to secure an analyst job will continue to be both exhilarating and challenging. The journey is riddled with ups and downs. Let us remember, that not being selected doesn't diminish our worth, and rejection might be guiding us toward a more fitting path.

Embrace setbacks, believe in yourself, and persistently work on building your personal brand. Your career trajectory is an evolving story, and each chapter contributes to your growth and success.

KEY TAKEAWAYS

In Chapter 3 we explored my journey to becoming a data analyst, starting from the growing need for data analysis in various industries. This chapter allowed me to reflect on my career path, initially transitioning from an assistant financial officer to a finance data analyst. More emphasis is on the importance of learning fundamental concepts such as math, programming, data wrangling, statistics, and databases, along with the significance of embracing big data analytics. My personal experiences highlight the value of practical experience, including volunteering for data projects and participating in data hackathons. We concluded by discussing the evolving job market and the significance of continuous learning and personal development for data analysts. Here are some key takeaways from this chapter:

1. **Growing Need for Data Analysis:** The demand for data analysis has increased with the rise of smartphones and other portable devices, leading to the collection of more data and the need for better and faster data analysis.

2. **Transitioning to Data Analysis:** Many individuals entered the field of data analysis out of necessity, with formal training not initially required. Various titles, such as business analyst and data analyst, were used to describe individuals responsible for managing data at different levels.

3. **Learning Fundamental Concepts:** Aspiring data analysts should focus on learning math fundamentals, programming languages (e.g., Python, VBA, SQL), data wrangling techniques, statistics, and databases. These foundational skills are essential for effective data analysis.

4. **Embracing Big Data Analytics:** Big data analytics involves advanced methods and tools to collect, process, and analyse large and diverse data sets. Learning big data concepts, such as working with Hadoop and other big data technologies, can be beneficial.

5. **Practical Experience:** Hands-on experience is crucial for retaining and applying data analysis skills effectively. Seeking opportunities to work on real data projects at work or participating in data hackathons can provide valuable experience.

6. **Learning Machine Learning:** Machine learning is a critical area for data analysts, involving supervised and unsupervised learning, time series analysis, and dimensionality reduction techniques.

7. **Finding Ways to Practice:** Practicing data analysis skills is essential for proficiency. While online resources are available, seeking hands-on experience through challenging projects at work or data hackathons can be more beneficial for some individuals.

8. **Navigating the Job Market:** The job market for data analysts has evolved, with more business leaders understanding the value of data analytics. Having a strong value proposition and showcasing skills through online platforms can enhance job opportunities.

9. **Continuous Learning:** Staying hungry for personal development and constant learning is crucial for data analysts. Continuous learning allows for growth and the acquisition of new skills to stay relevant in the field.

10. **Overcoming Challenges:** Pursuing a career in data analysis may come with challenges, including learning complex concepts and facing self-doubt. Joining a community of like-minded individuals can provide support and encouragement.

11. **Fresh Starts and Opportunities:** Regardless of previous experiences or backgrounds, individuals can start learning data analysis and coding at any time. Math or science subjects are not prerequisites for success in data analytics.

12. **Building a Supportive Tribe:** Finding a supportive community or group of friends who share similar career aspirations can be valuable in helping each other succeed in the data analytics field.

Overall, the chapter emphasizes the importance of foundational learning, continuous growth, and practical experience for aspiring data analysts. It encourages individuals to take bold moves, seek opportunities for hands-on practice, and build a strong foundation in data analysis to excel in their careers.

chapter 4

WHAT IS DATA SCIENCE? IS IT SYNONYMOUS WITH BUSINESS INTELLIGENCE?

I used to believe that any work involving data, regardless of its size or algorithms used, could be considered data science. However, after taking my big data module, I was left feeling confused. I thought that simply learning about big data and Hadoop file systems would make me a true data scientist, but during a group technology podcast, my mentor, who is also the Chief Data Officer (CDO) at the bank, revealed that many Business Intelligence (BI) professionals are falsely presenting themselves as data scientists. She emphasized the importance of thoroughly screening candidates during the hiring process to ensure that only true data scientists are hired. This is because hiring someone with the wrong skillset could result in delayed projects and unmet expectations, which can be costly. Therefore, it is better to take the time to find the right candidate rather than rushing to fill a position.

This bothered me a lot and I finally decided to enrol for data science and machine learning fundamentals. It was an online course provided by the Corporate Finance Institute (CFI)[35] for a fee. I decided to start with the free version and was immediately blown away. It never occurred to me that data science was all about the creation of data-driven insights that help organisations deal with uncertainty. The type of questions it aims to answer includes what type of customers are most likely to buy. What type of market regime is being entered? How much stock should be ordered to meet the forecast next week? Or when will the company run out of warehouse stock? Looking at the above questions it is unclear why there is such a fuss between BI and data science.

BI VS DATA SCIENCE

The best answer I have received thus far is that the difference is in the time frame. BI looks at past behaviour or trends. This is an equivalent of descriptive analytics where there is a need to understand what has taken place in the past. Data science, on the other hand, uses past observations (descriptive data) to make predictions, estimations, and decisions about the future. Based on

[35] Learn Data Science | Corporate Finance Institute - CFI offers a range of courses that can help you prepare for the fascinating world of Data Science. No matter whether you are a beginner or an expert in this field, gaining knowledge about the concepts of Data Science and Machine Learning is essential for advancing your skills.

this, we are likely to find BI analysts in teams that deal with reporting analytics. Data scientists are likely to be associated with value analytics and quantitative analytics where predictions need to be made within expectable risk parameters. All of this depends on the types of analysis needed from the team.

TYPES OF ANALYSIS

There are four types of analysis: descriptive, predictive, diagnostic, and prescriptive. Data scientists focus on predictive and prescriptive analysis because prescriptive analysis helps determine the best course of action to achieve a goal, while predictive analysis provides insight into future outcomes or unknown variables. On the other hand, BI uses data to understand past events and answer questions like "who," "where," "when," "how many," or "what" through descriptive analysis. Diagnostic analysis is relevant to both data science and BI analysis because it helps identify the root cause of a problem. Which type of analysis one chooses to focus on depends on their particular skill set.

DOMAIN OF KNOWLEDGE

To be an ideal data scientist, it is important to have expertise in three areas: (1) statistics and analysis, (2) computer science and coding, and (3) domain knowledge. Possessing proficiency in only two of these areas would not suffice to be an effective data scientist. For instance, having skills in statistics and analysis along with domain knowledge would classify you as a data analyst rather than a data scientist. Similarly, having expertise in domain knowledge, computer science and coding would make you a software developer and not a data scientist candidate. However, if you know computer science and statistics and analysis, you would be well-suited for machine learning and robotic process automation (RPA). Therefore, education and training, as well as work experience, play a crucial role in determining whether one is likely to be a data scientist.

DATA SCIENCE PROCESS

Not all insights are for reporting/decision-making purposes, some might be needed as part of operations. Data scientists navigate this journey with a meticulous eye for detail, a persistent quest for insights, and a steadfast commitment to transforming raw data into strategic decision-making tools. The product of the data science journey is not merely a structure of numbers and graphs, but an edifice of insight and knowledge that can guide the future course of a business.

The five-stage process of data science is a dynamic and intricate journey, one that begins with data collection and ends with sharing insights. The first stage starts with capturing data/information, ensuring the quality of data, and storing data in a database. This is followed by the need to optimise the data as the project dictates and select features of interest. Statistical and predictive analysis, as a third stage, requires us to build models and algorithms that spot patterns in the project data or features of interest. Once models have been created and completed, it is time to test how these models are performing. This fourth stage also allows us to start visualising what we get from models. Once we are happy with what has been tested, we then commence with the final stage of sharing insights using dashboards or reports with top management (Exco/Manco).

1. Data Collection and Storage: The Foundation Stone

The data scientist's initial task at hand is the collection and storage of data. This process can be equated to laying the cornerstone for a grand structure, the integrity of which is contingent on the quality and accuracy of this foundational element. In this phase, they meticulously capture a wide range of information. For instance, they might collect transactional data, usernames, and credit history, all while identifying instances of past fraud. Once gathered, these scientists strive to ensure the quality of the data and store it in the database securely, establishing the cornerstone of our structure.

2. Transform Data for Projects: Sculpting the Raw Stone

Having laid the foundation, data scientists then turn their attention to transforming and optimizing the data to suit the specific project they're tackling. It's akin to a master sculptor chiselling away at a raw stone, refining it into a meticulously crafted masterpiece. In this phase, they might find themselves merging datasets, filtering out irrelevant items, adjusting the format, or selecting specific features of interest. The goal is to shape the raw data into a form that best aligns with the project objectives.

3. Statistical & Predictive Analysis: The Architect's Blueprint

The stage of statistical and predictive analysis can be thought of as the blueprints drawn by an architect. Here, data analysts construct models and algorithms, creating a blueprint that reveals patterns within our data. For example, data scientists might train a model to identify the leading indicators of fraudulent transactions. This model serves as their compass, directing them towards the insights that they seek within the labyrinth of raw data. It forms the analytical engine that powers our data-driven insights.

4. Model Evaluation & Data Visualisation: Assessing the Structure

Once the analytical engine is operational, these scientists turn to the task of evaluating model performance. This is akin to an architect assessing a building structure for any potential weak points. Alongside this, they also translate our findings into visually compelling formats for easy understanding. The data scientist's goal in this stage is to answer questions like, "Which model is most effective at identifying fraudulent transactions?" and "How can we optimise our model to align with business objectives?" This dual assessment of functionality and performance ensures that their data science process remains aligned with the real-world objectives it seeks to serve.

5. Share Insights: Unveiling the Structure to the World

The final stage of the process is the sharing of insights. This stage could be likened to the unveiling of a grand architectural masterpiece to the world, where our data science model is put into action, and its insights are shared with business users. Here, they might provide dashboards and reports to decision-makers, aiding them in their strategic planning. They may also deploy our models into operations, sharing real-time information about risky transactions. This stage is the culmination of our process, where the fruits of our labour are finally harvested and shared.

UNDERSTANDING THE IMPACT OF DATA MODELS ON ORGANISATIONAL DECISION-MAKING

In today's data-driven world, data science models play a crucial role in shaping organisational decision-making. This is why ensuring the data team adheres to the data science process becomes a crucial part of decision-making. I have taken a lot of time explaining, especially to novice analysts, the importance of data - not only today but in the future. Thus as a novice analyst or a veteran polishing their skills, understanding the significance of model evaluation and its implications on business priorities is essential. I aim to shed some light on the importance of data science model evaluation from a leadership's (Exco/Manco) perspective, emphasizing alignment between business leaders and data science teams to achieve successful outcomes. We will explore the key aspects that top management (Exco/Manco) should consider when evaluating data models, including model objectives, limitations, and evaluation metrics.

1. Model Evaluation: The Foundation of Data Science Projects

Model evaluation is the cornerstone of data science projects from an Exco/Manco standpoint. It involves assessing the performance and accuracy of predictive models to determine their effectiveness in achieving business objectives. Exco/Manco must actively engage with data science teams to align priorities, objectives, and measures of success. By understanding model outputs and their impact on decision-making, leaders can make well-informed choices to drive the organisation forward.

2. Collaboration Between Business Leaders (Exco/Manco) and Data Science Teams

For a data science project to be successful, Exco/Manco and data science teams must collaborate closely. The data scientists, analysts, and engineers solve the technical challenges and select the best analytical approaches, while Exco/Manco provides insight into an overall organisational strategy, business objectives, project goals, and associated costs. This collaboration ensures that the models are developed to deliver targeted value to the business, enabling better decision-making based on data-driven insights.

3. Defining Model Objectives and Target Outcomes

At the outset of any data science project, it is crucial to define clear model objectives and target outcomes. Exco/Manco must articulate why a specific model is being built and what business value it aims to deliver. For instance, when dealing with fraud detection, it is essential to quantify the cost of false alarms and the benefits of correct identification. By understanding these factors, leaders can align efforts to optimize the model's performance and reduce false alarms or missed fraudulent activity.

4. Recognizing Model Limitations and Resource Allocation

It is essential to acknowledge that no data science model can achieve 100% accuracy. As we strive for higher accuracy, the costs in terms of time and resources tend to increase exponentially. Exco/Manco must work closely with data science teams to set realistic expectations and allocate resources efficiently. By understanding the model's limitations, leaders can make informed decisions about when to stop pursuing higher accuracy and when to focus resources on other aspects of the project.

5. Evaluation Metrics: Understanding the Implications

Evaluation metrics are essential in assessing the model's performance and effectiveness. Two crucial concepts to grasp are (1) False Positives, False Negatives, True Positives, and True Negatives, and (2) Regression Coefficients.

Here is a brief explanation of each:

1. False Positives, False Negatives, True Positives, and True Negatives:

    a. **False Positives**: Instances where the model predicts a positive outcome, but the actual result is negative. Let us assume this is like having spam/junk emails going through your inbox. We must teach the model about this error by reclassification.

b. **False Negatives**: Instances where the model predicts a negative outcome, but the actual result is positive. It is like finding your important email falsely categorised as spam/junk email.
c. **True Positives**: Instances where the model predicts a positive outcome, and the actual result is also positive. Having all the emails you want in your inbox without misclassifications.
d. **True Negatives**: Instances where the model predicts a negative outcome, and the actual result is also negative. Yep, junk is junk is junk.

2. Regression Coefficients: Regression coefficients represent the weight given to each input feature in the model. Positive coefficients indicate a positive correlation with the target variable, while negative coefficients indicate a negative correlation.

There is tons of information on how data science models continue to play a crucial role in shaping organisational decision-making. Data science model evaluation is a critical process for business leaders (Exco/Manco) to understand and prioritise effectively. By aligning objectives, acknowledging limitations, and comprehending evaluation metrics, leaders can make informed decisions that drive business success.

We have successfully explored the key aspects that Exco/Manco should consider. Let us all remember that a successful data science project delivers targeted value to the organisation and empowers better decision-making based on accurate, data-driven insights. As a novice analyst, mastering these concepts will pave the way for your growth and impact as a data-driven professional. The question in mind now could be "What is machine learning and how does it relate to data analysis/science?"

UNDERSTANDING MACHINE LEARNING AND DATA SCIENCE MODELS

Data science and machine learning have revolutionized the way we analyse and interpret vast amounts of data. This became evident the minute I set foot in the big data class. Although I didn't major in statistics or mathematics like my computer science peers, I knew that knowing data discovery and manipulation is the path most organisations will be heading to. Machine learning (ML), commonly known as artificial intelligence (AI), and data science will be the most sought-after skills for the coming decade. This is irrespective of the industry or sector.

These fields offer powerful techniques and models that can extract valuable insights and make predictions. We will continue to explore the exciting world of data science and delve into the different types of machine learning that form the foundation of this field. Whether you're a non-technical novice analyst or simply curious about data science, this guide will provide a comprehensive overview of the key models and their applications. But first, let me explain a little bit about ML.

Types of Machine Learning (ML)

There are two types of ML namely, supervised machine learning and unsupervised machine learning. Let us discuss each separately.

Supervised ML: Supervised machine learning involves training models using labelled data, where each data point is associated with a known output or target value. Think of it as carefully looking after a growing baby. Well, that is if the baby could grow as fast as the machine learns. This type of learning is extremely fast depending on processing power. The learnings enable the model to learn patterns and relationships to predict outcomes for new, unseen data. I guess this to be likened to when a baby starts telling you things you never thought about before. Furthermore, there are two types of supervised ML which are as follows.

- *Regression*: Regression is a supervised learning technique for predicting continuous numeric values. We can benefit from regressions by having at least thirty consecutive data points. This is achieved by analysing the relationship between input features and a continuous target variable; regression models can estimate values such as housing prices, stock prices, or sales figures. Regression is an excellent measure to show how closely related each variable is. A higher regression number tells us that all the variables explain almost all changes in the variable under observation. We will have a special chapter to discuss regression in detail
- *Classification*: Classification is another supervised learning approach that predicts discrete class labels. In this

method, the model learns to identify patterns in input features and assign data points to predefined classes. We as humans do this naturally. We find it easy to look at our co-workers and we can classify almost everything about them. Computers are now being taught how to do this classification just as well as we can. Classification models are commonly used for spam detection, sentiment analysis, and disease diagnosis. Imagine how your email inbox would look without any classification/spam detection algorithm.

Unsupervised Machine Learning: I know that this sounds like a naughty child using a permanent maker on your walls, but the reality is less exciting than this. Unsupervised machine learning involves exploring data without any predefined labels or target variables. It's like saying play soccer the whole day without goalposts. Instead, the goal is to uncover hidden patterns, group similar data points, or reduce the dimensionality of the data. Imagine scoring a goal by passing a ball to teammates, throwing the ball, and all other undefined moves. Before we get too excited, we have two types I want to focus on.

- *Clustering*: Clustering is an unsupervised learning technique that groups similar data points based on their similarities or proximity in the input feature space. Clustering algorithms, such as K-means or hierarchical clustering, are employed in customer segmentation, image segmentation, and anomaly detection. I used clustering, as part of my assignment, on world economic data to group countries based on seventeen variables over two decades.

- *Variable Reduction*: Variable reduction, also known as dimensionality reduction, aims to reduce the number of input features while preserving important information. Techniques like principal component analysis (PCA) or feature selection methods help identify the most relevant features, simplify the data, and improve model performance. Imagine how difficult it would be if you had two hundred variables to describe you. If someone asks me about you, they might get an hour-long description. But as humans, we are quick to pick contextually important variables and then use them to describe a person. Variable reduction is not variable elimination but rather reducing two hundred variables to a few key variables.

Types of Other ML Models

Various models could be used in ML. For illustration purposes, let's describe it as a syllabus. As parents, we like to brag about our kids' education which boils down to the syllabus they are being taught. The syllabus could be any of the approved South African ones like CAPS, IEB, or Cambridge Education. Likewise, computers use various ways to learn. Let us focus on the types of other ML models like reinforcement learning and neural networks & deep learning.

- *Reinforcement Learning*: Reinforcement learning focuses on training an agent to make sequential decisions in an environment to maximize a cumulative reward. It's like teaching your dog not to relieve himself in the house but instead go outside and use a dedicated spot. We reward the dog for good and acceptable behaviour and punish it for undesirable ones. Likewise, reinforcement learning is where the agent interacts with the environment, receives feedback through rewards or penalties, and learns optimal strategies. This type of learning is used in robotics, game-playing, and autonomous systems. All we aim for is more good behaviour and less of the undesirable.

- *Neural Networks & Deep Learning*: Neural networks are inspired by the structure and function of the human brain. Deep learning, a subfield of machine learning, utilizes neural networks with multiple layers. This approach has gained significant attention due to its remarkable success in image recognition, natural language processing, and speech synthesis tasks.

Types of Other Data Science Models

Now that we have discussed ML above, it is befitting for us to discuss data science. Not just the complete discipline, but rather the models that are being used. For this discussion, I would like us to focus on (1) Monte Carlo simulation, (2) Rule-based modelling, and (3) other statistical models.

- *Monte Carlo Simulation*: Monte Carlo simulation leverages random sampling and statistical analysis to model and simulate complex systems. By running multiple simulations with varying input parameters, this technique estimates the behaviour and uncertainty of a system. Monte Carlo simulation finds applications in finance, engineering, and risk analysis. We were advised to use this for scenario planning in project finance. This is a perfect tool to help you change the scenarios and instantly see what impact each scenario would have in the future. I use the word scenario planning and not forecasting, deliberately.

- *Rule-Based Models*: Rule-based models, or expert systems, utilize predefined rules or logical statements to make decisions or solve problems. These models encode human expertise or domain-specific knowledge to reason and infer outcomes. Rule-based models are employed in medical diagnosis, fault detection, and recommendation systems.

Other Statistical Models: Beyond machine learning, data science incorporates a wide range of statistical models. Linear regression, logistic regression, time series analysis, Bayesian models, and many other techniques provide the foundation for understanding relationships between variables, making predictions, and drawing meaningful inferences. Learning R and Python could be beneficial to us in applying statistical techniques for improved analysis. All of the above depend on the role you will be fulfilling in the data science team. If that is so, the question to ask could be “What are all the roles involved in data science?”

DATA SCIENCE ROLES

There are seven different roles in the field of data science, each requiring a specific set of skills. When hiring a data science team, managers may consider which roles are needed for the team's objectives. Understanding these roles can help individuals identify which tasks they may already be working on and what steps they can take to progress in their careers. Furthermore, the different roles in data science can help individuals identify their strengths and opportunities for growth in the field.

Over the past few decades, the computer science field has continued to grow. According to the US Bureau of Labour Statistics, information and computer science research jobs are growing at 21% by 2031[36], which is much faster than the average for all other occupations. Understanding the data science team would thus give a competitive edge in selecting an area of interest especially given how young the field is. Online courses like the Business Intelligence & Data Analysis course (BIDA)[37] offered by the Corporate Finance Institute play a crucial role in demystifying this field and choosing a role in the data science team.

Data science roles can vary greatly in specialisation, so it's important to carefully review job descriptions. Some roles may focus on data collection and storage, such as a Data Architect. Others may involve transforming data for analysis, such as a Data Engineer/SQL Developer or Database Admin. Roles like Data Analyst may require skills in statistics, predictive analysis, and model evaluation. A Data Visualisation Specialist may focus on

---

[36] Computer and Information Technology Occupations : Occupational Outlook Handbook: : U.S. Bureau of Labor Statistics (bls.gov) - Overall employment in computer and information technology occupations is projected to grow 15 percent from 2021 to 2031, much faster than the average for all occupations; this increase is expected to result in about 682,800 new jobs over the decade. In addition to new jobs from growth, opportunities arise from the need to replace workers who leave their occupations permanently. About 418,500 openings each year, on average, are projected to come from growth and replacement needs.

[37] Become a Certified Business Intelligence & Data Analyst (BIDA) (corporatefinanceinstitute.com) - CFI's Business Intelligence & Data Analyst Certification Program will teach you the most important skills required to kickstart or advance your data analysis career. Learn how to use the most popular business intelligence tools and programming languages to explore, understand, and master data science.

communicating insights through visualisations. The Data Scientist's role involves coding and analysis, with less emphasis on data collection and storage. Finally, the Machine Learning Engineers role requires proficiency in all stages of data science, including software and data engineering.

1. Data Architect

A data architect's duties are to create the data strategy including how, where, when, and what data is stored. They are IT professionals responsible for defining the policies, procedures, models, and technologies to be used in collecting, organizing, storing, and accessing company information according to TechTarget[38]. The position is often confused with a database architect and data engineer. However, data architects focus on high-level business intelligence relationships and data policies, whereas the previously mentioned positions handle the application of those relationships and policies to the design of specific databases. There are over four hundred data architect vacancies listed on LinkedIn[39] in South Africa and over three thousand on Pnet[40]. This shows the high demand for data architects in our country.

The primary task is to drive and transform the data capabilities and enable a data-driven culture across the group and therefore work with other architects and platform teams to ensure data is managed as an asset in a centralized, standardized, and consistent manner to maintain consistency and quality, using

[38] What is a Data Architect and How Do You Become One? (techtarget.com)

[39] https://www.linkedin.com/jobs/data-architect-jobs?originalSubdomain=za

[40] Data Architect jobs in South Africa | Pnet

mature technologies and emerging data practices. The data architect role requires an understanding of various data management and processing-related technologies and choices, has a deep understanding of both SQL/No-SQL technologies, distributed computing framework, and techniques to make the right tool and technology choices.

2. Data Engineer

According to Coursera[41], data engineers work in a variety of settings to build systems that collect, manage, and convert raw data into usable information for data scientists and business analysts to interpret. Their goal is to make data accessible so that organisations can use it to evaluate and optimize their performance. They are one of the more technical roles in the business intelligence (BI) or data science process. This is because they ensure data quality & availability of data and queries and ensure that analysts have what they need to do their job. There is a professional data engineer certification offered by Google[42] to allow enthusiasts to design, build, operationalise, secure, and monitor data processing systems with a particular emphasis on security and compliance; scalability and efficiency; reliability and fidelity; and flexibility and portability.

3. Data Analysts

A data analyst gathers, cleans, and studies data sets to help solve problems. They do this by focusing on the analysis that we all are

[41] What Is a Data Engineer?: A Guide to This In-Demand Career | Coursera

[42] Get Certified Program 2023 (inthecloud.withgoogle.com)

most familiar with, sourcing data, formulas, data models, pivot tables, and visuals. They also understand the business well and search for insights derived from data. Data analysts work in many industries, including business, finance, criminal justice, science, medicine, and government. Some common tools they use include Microsoft Excel, Google Sheets, SQL, Tableau, R or Python, SAS, Microsoft Power BI and sometimes Jupyter Notebooks. Anyone can become a data analyst irrespective of whether you have a university qualification or not. You need to have these technical skills; Database tools (Microsoft Excel and SQL), Programming languages (Python or R), Data visualization (Tableau, Power BI, Jupyter Notebook, and Excel), and Statistics and mathematics concepts.

4. Database Administrator (DBA)

According to Oracle[43], a DBA is responsible for maintaining, securing, and operating databases and ensuring that data is correctly stored and retrieved. In addition, DBAs often work with developers to design and implement new features and troubleshoot any issues. A DBA must have a strong understanding of both technical and business needs. There are different types of DBA's depending on specific duties and responsibilities.

A DBA could be any of the following:

- System administrators are responsible for the overall management and upkeep of a computer system, including

[43] What is a database administrator (DBA)? | Oracle

installing and configuring software, applying security patches, and monitoring system performance.

- Data modellers who create and maintain data models that depict the relationship between data elements. Data modelling is a critical component of effective database design.
- Application DBAs are responsible for administrating databases that support applications. Specific tasks include installing and configuring applications, ensuring that data is synchronized correctly between databases, and troubleshooting application-related issues.
- Task-oriented DBAs focus on a particular area of database administration, such as backup and recovery, security, or performance tuning. They typically have in-depth knowledge of a specific Database Management System (DBMS).
- Performance analysts monitor database performance and identify areas where improvement is needed. They may also be responsible for creating performance reports and providing recommendations to database administrators.
- Data warehouse administrators manage databases that store data for business intelligence or decision-support applications. They are responsible for extracting data correctly, transforming the data, and loading it into the data warehouse.
- Cloud DBAs are responsible for administrating databases hosted in a cloud computing environment, provisioning and managing database instances, setting up replication and high availability, and monitoring database performance.

5. Data Visualization Specialist

The data visualisation specialist turns insights into meaningful visuals that drive action. They also understand how the business works and how people think thus communication skills are vital to their success. Some job responsibilities could include: collaborating with internal teams to build and customize individual client reporting dashboards; managing the internal dashboard ticketing process and working with teams to resolve errors; assisting with dashboarding projects, including data connections, business requirements, and setup; Train team members on new and existing processes and best practices; developing and maintain SQL data extracts, scheduled jobs, API integrations, and views; working with client teams and subject matter experts to strategize on data-driven business process improvements; transition Excel-based reporting to automated and standardized solutions; communicating with data visualisation vendors and troubleshoot dashboard and platform issues. They could also provide input and recommendations on new potential data management solutions based on research and analysis.

6. Data Scientist

Data scientists are focused on coding for analysis. They are expected to be proficient in advanced statistical methods and coding, which are used to create analyses and predictions from data. A data scientist's duties can include developing strategies for analysing data, preparing data for analysis, exploring, analysing, and visualizing data, building models with data using programming languages, such as Python and R, and deploying models into applications. The data scientist doesn't work alone but rather works in teams using platforms that allow them to achieve advanced analytics. According to Oracle, data scientist platforms should be chosen based on: (1) project-based UI that encourages collaboration, (2) prioritized integration and flexibility (support from tools such as GitHub, GitLab, and Bitbucket, and tight integration with other resources), (3) inclusion of enterprise-grade capabilities, (4) making data science more self-service, and (5) ensuring easier model deployment.

As a speciality, data science is young. It grew out of the fields of statistical analysis and data mining. The Data Science Journal debuted in 2002, published by the *International Council for Science: Committee on Data for Science and Technology.* By 2008 the title of data scientist had emerged, and the field quickly took off[44]. There has been a shortage of data scientists ever since, even though more and more colleges and universities have started offering data science degrees.

7. Machine Learning Engineer

Machine learning is a part of the computer science field specifically concerned with artificial intelligence. It uses algorithms to interpret data in a way that replicates how humans learn. Machine learning engineers act as critical members of the data science team. Their tasks involve researching, building, and designing the artificial intelligence responsible for machine learning and maintaining and improving existing artificial intelligence systems. They are expected to integrate analysis and predictive models into real-world systems, apps, or websites.

---

[44] Data science - Wikipedia

They could also link models with automated data feeds that often update in real time. Machine learning engineers will likely know several coding languages and have a highly technical skillset. While the job requirements are not universal, some might include implementing machine learning algorithms, Running AI systems experiments and tests, Designing and developing machine learning systems, and performing statistical analyses.

KEY TAKEAWAYS

The chapter started with clearing up any confusion about the definition of data science, particularly after taking a look at big data. To clarify: not all work involving data can be considered data science. One of my mentors - Chief Data Officer (CDO) at one of the big five South African banks - emphasized the need to differentiate true data scientists from business intelligence (BI) professionals.

Here are the key takeaways for us from this chapter:

1. **BI vs. Data Science:** We have explained the difference between business intelligence and data science. BI focuses on past behaviour or trends using descriptive analytics, while data science uses past observations to make predictions, estimations, and decisions about the future using predictive and prescriptive analysis.

2. **Types of Analysis**: There are four types of analysis: descriptive, predictive, diagnostic, and prescriptive. Data scientists focus on predictive and prescriptive analysis, while BI analysts deal with descriptive and diagnostic analysis, depending on the team's needs.

3. **The domain of Knowledge**: To be an ideal data scientist, expertise in three areas is crucial: statistics and analysis, computer science and coding, and domain knowledge. Having skills in only two of these areas would classify one

as a data analyst or a software developer, but not a data scientist.

4. **Data Science Process**: The data science process is explained in five stages: data collection and storage, transforming data for projects, statistical and predictive analysis, model evaluation and data visualization, and sharing insights with business leaders (Exco/Manco).

5. **Data Models on Organisational Decision-Making**: This section emphasizes the importance of model evaluation in data science projects. Business leaders (Exco/Manco) must actively engage with data science teams to align priorities and objectives. Clear model objectives, target outcomes, and understanding model limitations and resource allocation are essential for successful decision-making.

6. **Machine Learning and Data Science Models**: We explored the world of data science and delved into the different types of machine learning: supervised (regression, classification) and unsupervised (clustering, variable reduction). The section also touches on other data science models like reinforcement learning, neural networks, deep learning, Monte Carlo simulation, rule-based models, and statistical models.

This chapter provides a comprehensive understanding of data science:- the differences between business intelligence, the key models used in data science and machine learning, and their impact on organisational decision-making. It aims to help readers grasp the significance of data-driven insights in today's data-driven world and the role of data scientists in providing valuable information for decision-making.

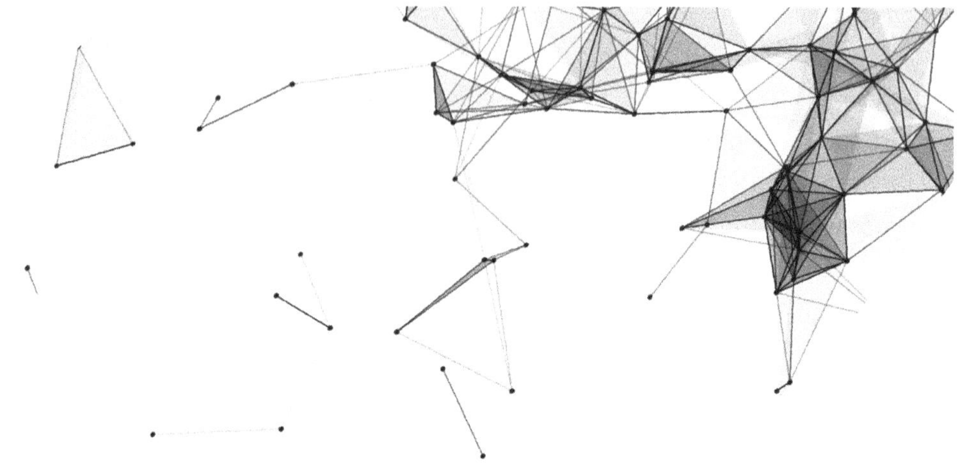

chapter 5

WHAT IS BUSINESS INTELLIGENCE? – UNDERSTANDING ANALYST ROLES AND TEAM MANAGEMENT

Understanding Business Intelligence (BI) allows us to demystify and differentiate from data science. In my experience, business intelligence allows for better information access for management and improved reporting. We know from the previous chapter that BI is well-suited for descriptive and diagnostic analysis. Descriptive analysis helps us understand “who”, “where”, “when”, "how many", or "what" happened in the past as shown by the data. Diagnostic analysis tells us why something is happening (the leading cause). When I started my career in a finance department in 2008, we relied much on management information systems (MIS). This finance MIS introduced me to analysis and I later fell in love with Data-Driven Insights (DDI). DDI better serves the organisation and teams when we improve MIS departments to focus on BI. But before we start to think that MIS is outdated, we must understand what BI is and why is it important in the organisation.

WHAT IS BUSINESS INTELLIGENCE (BI)

BI could be defined as the practice of turning data into actionable insights. This definition allows us to distinguish BI from others by processes, tools, skills, and roles. The main objective of business intelligence is to provide actionable insights that enable senior management and business leaders to change or maintain a course of action. I am stating specifically that BI works best for senior management and business executives (top management) as we tend to require operational insights and reports for middle and lower management. It is better to invest in BI if you are battling with readily available insights for decision-making. Otherwise, it would be more beneficial to invest in report optimisation for operational reports using Robotics Process Automation (RPA)[45] instead of BI.

[45] What is Robotic Process Automation - RPA Software | UiPath - Robotic process automation (RPA) is a software technology that allows the creation, deployment, and management of software robots that can act like humans when interacting with digital systems and software. These robots can perform various tasks such as understanding the contents on a screen, typing the right keys,

KEY SKILLS REQUIRED FOR BI

To be successful in Business Intelligence (BI), it's important to have strong skills in statistics and analysis. This can be broken down into four key areas:

- Basic statistics (descriptive statistics),
- Data transformation,
- Data visualization, and
- Business knowledge.

While BI analysts don't necessarily need to have expertise in a specific industry, understanding company operations is crucial. BI analysts focus on analysing past trends and identifying current ones, on a daily basis. As a former Senior Financial Business Analyst, I often received questions about IT headcount growth concerning transformation goals and year-to-date financial actuals compared to forecasts. To answer these questions, different team members would provide valuable insights. Knowing that different team members are involved, your question now could be “How many roles are involved in the BI process?” with a follow-up question being “Are BI roles the same as data science roles?”

BI ROLES AND RESPONSIBILITIES

Different roles can be included as part of the BI analysis. This includes data engineers, data business & process analysts, data analysts, data visualisation specialists, and team leaders or senior

---

navigating systems, extracting data, and executing several defined actions. Unlike humans, software robots can perform these tasks continuously, accurately, and without the need for breaks or rest.

managers who would assist with decision-making. Data visualisation specialists are team members who help with visuals, reporting and dashboards. They will be using data models that were developed by data analysts. Data analysts best make data models and analyses that are optimised for visualisation. Data engineers prepare data for data analysts as they specialise in data storage and ETL (Extract, Transform, and Load) procedures. We can see there might be similar roles in data science and thus important for us to make a distinction.

DISTINGUISHING BUSINESS INTELLIGENCE ROLES FROM DATA SCIENCE ROLES

Previously, there was no need for various roles in data. When the data guys inducted me into data in 2009 there wasn't much buzz about BI then. To affirm this, all they told me was that I only needed to know a few SQL scripts and would be ready to go. They trusted me with databases, knowing they had backups from the data warehouse. It was in 2017 that I started to notice the importance of having different data roles. Maybe this was driven by the fact that I had moved from the unsecured lending operations team and was now in the Group Technology (GT) Finance department working closely with the Data-Driven Intelligence (DDI) team. The DDI team was so big because it consolidated all the data professionals from the entire bank. They were then divided into roles. The team also arranged themselves into squads so that there could be a better focus.

Each squad would comprise each BI role. This means that each squad would have as many data engineers as possible, data analysts, business/process analysts, and Power BI visualisation specialists. The squads were arranged this way to enable speciality and focus on data. Credit card data and overdrafts, insurance, personal loans, and so forth had its squad. More squads would depend on the team's growth and business needs. Once we have discussed the overview composition of the BI department, it is also important to understand what is expected from (1) data engineers, (2) data analysts, and (3) visualisation specialists.

Data Engineer

Data engineers source, organize and move data between systems. They can also be involved in decisions about data storage and infrastructure. Their key competencies include:

- *Extract, Transform, and Load (ETL)* to automate data feeds or migrate data from various systems, and
- *Data warehouse (DW)* creation to store all data needed by the business. DW helps data users access everything in one place/server thus less need to create ETL themselves – optimised for analysis,
- *Data Governance* is security-focused to ensure data integrity, and
- *Data system knowledge* especially mastering and understanding data structures and other ways to help analysts avoid data issues.

Data engineers know various types of database systems optimised both for computers and human analysis.

There are four types of database systems namely:

- Online Transaction Processing (OLTP),
- Data Lake,
- Data Warehouse (DW), and Data Mart.

They could be distinguished as follows;

- **OLTP** is a type of data processing that consists of executing several transactions occurring concurrently i.e.: online banking, shopping, order entry, or sending text messages, for example. It is also optimized to enter, modify, delete, and read data.
- A **Data Lake** is a centralized repository designed to store, process, and secure large amounts of structured (tables and lists), semi-structured, and unstructured data (emails and phone conversations). It can store data in its native format and process any variety of it, ignoring size limits.
- A **DW** is a type of data management system that is designed to enable and support BI activities, especially analytics. It combines data from multiple sources. DWs are solely intended to perform queries and analysis often contain large amounts of historical data and are optimized for analysis and human interaction.
- A **Data Mart** is a simple form of a data warehouse that is focused on a single subject or line of business, such as sales, finance, or marketing. Given their focus, data marts draw data from fewer sources than data warehouses. This makes data marts ideal for small data warehouses used for a specific project (squad) or team.

The ideal programming language used is Structured Query Language (SQL). SQL is ideal to query and fetch data from databases. It is easy to read and write using SQL. There are various online resources catered for novice programmers to be proficient in SQL. My personal favourite has always been SQL Tutorial (w3schools.com)[46]. I found W3Schools.com to be more elaborate especially considering that databases and SQL language were only covered in two chapters of the software engineering book[47]. The main objective might have been for us to seek help online as novice programmers rather than relying on the textbook for everything. Knowing SQL might seem a bit primitive to today's analysts, but an understanding of SQL will set you apart from dashboard-focused BI analysts, especially when considering all the various tools that assist with analysis.

The common tools used by data engineers include tools for data storage, cloud services, coding languages, big data manipulation, and live stream data. There are various ways to store data, which include Microsoft server management studios, Oracle, SAP, SAS, and other data storage tools. There have been improvements following the increasing cost of physical data storage and reduced speed of query (latency[48]) to have an online solution to data storage. Providers such as Google Cloud Storage (GCS), Microsoft Azure, and Amazon Web Services (AWS) have filled this need. Data engineers are welcome to use any of the

[46] SQL Tutorial (w3schools.com) - SQL is a standard language for storing, manipulating and retrieving data in databases. This SQL tutorial will teach you how to use SQL in: MySQL, SQL Server, MS Access, Oracle, Sybase, Informix, Postgres, and other database systems.

[47] Ian Sommerville, Software Engineering, 9/e, Published: 2011, ISBN:9788131762165, 8131762165

[48] Latency is the delay before a transfer of data begins following an instruction for its transfer

programming/coding languages such as SQL, Scala, or Python with either local or online data storage providers. Some providers have specialisation in big data manipulation which varies a little to SQL, Python and Scala. These include Hadoop, Sparks, and Databricks for big data that is not live streaming. Live streaming data could be handled using Kafta, Pubsub, Kenesis DS, or Apache Beam. I am not much of an expert in big data manipulation and live stream data except for completing one assignment in university. I have been relating more to data analysis in my analysis roles. Now that we know so much about data engineers, we still need to know "What would data analysts do?"

Data Analysts

Data analysts are responsible for building data models and metrics, which facilitate analysis and visualization. Like data engineers, they are specialists in (1) ETL to import data from Excel files, CSV files and databases, transform data into the desired format, and load data into models, (2) Calculate matrices by writing formulae that calculate business performances thus requiring a good understanding of data, (3) Creating data models which require them to combine tables that link related data together and do it to refresh automatically, (4) Documentation of data models for other analysts as well as all the metric definitions using a data dictionary. They can make use of tools to achieve the above tasks.

The common tools used by data analysts include traditional ones like Microsoft Excel, VBA, and Access. Other data transformation tools include SQL server management and Power Query (Excel 2016 and later). Besides this, they can make use of the following tools: Tableau, Power Pivot, or Power BI for advanced analysis. Other popular tools include QliK, R, and Python. Data analysts could team up with data visualisation specialists to focus on data modelling while others work on building dashboards and interactive analysis. This means that in an ideal team, a data analyst does not have to do anything related to the visualisation of data.

Data Visualisation Specialists

Data visualisation specialists focus on turning clean data into visuals that help communicate a message or help answer a specific question. Their key competencies include:

- *Creating data visuals* that highlight key data points or trends and also focus on one or a few metrics,
- *Creating dashboards* by combining multiple visuals into one, to tell a story using data & visuals (that enable others to see the detail and identify root causes),
- *Communicating results and presenting to audiences* in management meetings manage audience permissions (e.g. row-level security), and
- *Audience feedback* about ways to make the report clearer, how to ensure consistency, how to improve definitions etc.

As a Senior Finance Business Analyst, I used to conduct monthly sessions with the finance team where I shared knowledge and they also provided feedback. I realised quickly how many Finance Officers (FOs) benefit from knowing their problems are already solved by a dashboard. There are many tools in the market specially designed to help with visualisation tasks/dashboards.

The industry leaders in data visualisation include Tableau, Power BI, and Excel. Other tools are already making waves such are MicroStrategy, Qlik, Looker, Sisense, Dundas BI, Python, Adaptive Insights, Plotly or Analysis. The choice of tool is dependent on how the business leader (Management committee/Manco) wants to see the data and not on what is easier for the data team. Business leaders are the main audience of BI reports and dashboards. They are also key to guiding our data and analysis strategy. Data visualisation should assist with decision-making and allow top management to maintain or change the course of action. This sure sounds exciting especially if you are working in small teams or on a project. What you might ask is "How then are BI teams structured given many handovers?" or "Will the process followed be the same as the data science process?"

BI TEAMS

We can see from above that understanding BI allows us to differentiate it from data science. The processes followed are different to the ones followed by data scientists. This explains how a hiring manager would be able to pick up if the candidate is a data scientist or BI analyst. BI is best suited for descriptive analysis which helps business leaders understand "who", "where", "when", "how many", or "what" happened for better decision-making. In so doing, data is being transformed into actionable insights thus making BI a key partner for decision making.

There need to have various roles within the data department has become prevalent in recent years. There was little distinguishment when I joined in 2009 and soon realised that it becomes tougher for one person to do all tasks in a big team. This prompted the BI team to have roles like Data engineers, Data analysts, and Visualisation specialists. Having a great relationship between the data team and Manco allows the entire organisation to maintain or change the course of action. Being a key person in the Group Technology Finance Department and working so closely with Financial Officers eliminated all the red tape thus allowing for better decision-making.

You could imagine the burden on team managers to ensure that each piece of analysis is handed over to the appropriate role. Not having a well-coordinated approach could create chaos followed by project failures. This is why we see so many teams opt to use various project management methodologies. While we could avoid asking "How many project management methodologies are there?" we could rather focus on which ones could best assist the team deliver.

MANAGING BI TEAMS USING PROJECT MANAGEMENT METHODOLOGIES

Working closely with BI teams, I had an opportunity to see marvellous teamwork. We have all heard about Agile and lately Kanban in meeting rooms or team sessions that involved BI teams. Just like that, we all stole these new ways of working to manage team deliverables. In case you have been wondering where all these terms are coming from. The short answer is that they are project management methodologies. Project management is the process of applying specific knowledge, skills, tools, and techniques to plan, execute, and complete a project within a certain scope, time, and budget. Effective project management is essential for the successful execution of projects, ensuring that they are completed on time, within budget, and to the desired quality standards. Project management is important because it helps teams achieve their goals and solve problems more efficiently and effectively.

Some examples of project management could include developing new software for an improved business process, constructing a building or infrastructure, organizing a relief effort after a natural disaster, expanding sales into a new geographic market, and launching a new product or service. Various methodologies have emerged over the years to guide project teams in achieving these goals. I will provide a comprehensive overview of three prominent project management methodologies: Waterfall, Agile, and Kanban. We will delve into their key characteristics, advantages, disadvantages, and real-life success applications.

Waterfall Methodology

This methodology is a traditional and linear approach that follows a sequence of phases, such as requirements, design, implementation, verification, and maintenance. Each phase must be completed before the next one can start. This methodology is suitable for short and predictable BI projects with clear and fixed requirements. This is why the advantages of choosing this methodology include: clear structure - the phased approach offers a well-defined structure, making it easier to plan and manage;

comprehensive documentation is produced at each phase, ensuring a clear record of the project's progress; well-suited for stable requirements. When requirements are known and stable, Waterfall can be efficient. But there are also downsides to choosing this methodology.

The disadvantages of using the Waterfall method could include limited adaptability - any changes to requirements after the BI project has begun, can be challenging to accommodate; limited customer involvement due to feedback often received at the end of the project; and high risk of failure because of the initial requirements being misunderstood or miscommunicated. Furthermore, involving the customer later may lead to misalignment with expectations. The good news is that the Waterfall methodology has been successful in industries where regulatory compliance and documentation are crucial, such as manufacturing and aerospace. For instance, the development of medical devices often follows a Waterfall approach to ensure strict quality control and documentation.

Agile Methodology

Agile is an iterative and incremental methodology that emphasizes collaboration, flexibility, and customer involvement. It divides the BI project into smaller iterations, called sprints, where each iteration produces a usable deliverable. The advantages are adaptability, customer-centric, and continuous improvement. This is because Agile welcomes changes to requirements, allowing the BI project to adapt to evolving needs. Continuous customer involvement and feedback ensure that the product meets customer expectations. This is another good thing from the customer's point of view. Doing these customer sessions allows for regular retrospectives enabling teams to learn from each iteration and enhance their processes.

The disadvantages of Agile methodology are complex management, potential scope creep, and limited documentation. This is because the iterative nature can make project tracking and management more challenging. Besides, frequent changes to requirements can lead to scope creep if not managed effectively. While Agile encourages working software over documentation, some projects require comprehensive documentation. Agile is widely used in software development. One notable example is Spotify, which utilizes Agile principles to continuously deliver updates to its music streaming platform[49]. The ability to respond to user feedback and market trends has contributed to their success.

Kanban Methodology

Kanban is a methodology that helps teams and organisations manage and improve their work processes. It is based on the principles of visualising work, limiting work in progress, and continuously improving the flow and quality of work. Did you know that Kanban was originally developed by Toyota[50] in the 1940s to

[49] The Spotify Agile Model: Principles & Takeaways - GitScrum Skyrocket Productivity - The Spotify model is based on the following four principles: (1) Teams are autonomous and self-organizing; (2) Teams own the end-to-end delivery of value to users; (3) There is a strong focus on continuous delivery and learning; (4) Decisions are made based on data and evidence.

[50] Toyota Production System (TPS & Lean Manufacturing) | Creative Safety Supply - Kanban, the "Just-in-Time" manufacturing system of TPS is a strategy for scheduling in the manufacturing process. Rather than having a massive inventory of each part that is required for the products being

optimise its production system and reduce waste? The methodology was later adapted to software development and other knowledge. Kanban focuses on visualising the workflow, limiting Work In Progress (WIP), and achieving a continuous flow of tasks. It operates as a pull-based system, where work is pulled into the next phase only when capacity allows. Besides Toyota, in software development, Microsoft's Visual Studio Team Services used Kanban to manage their software projects. We can all get this feature in MS Teams[51]. By visualising workflow and managing WIP limits, better predictability and increased efficiency is achieved.

The advantages of choosing this methodology include flexibility, efficient flow, and continuous improvement. This is because Kanban optimises workflow by minimizing bottlenecks and ensuring tasks are completed in a timely manner. The workload is adjusted based on capacity, making it suitable for teams with variable workloads. Regularly analysing and adjusting the process improves efficiency over time thus making the team work better. The disadvantages are a lack of structure and limited long-term planning. Kanban's flexibility may easily lead to a lack of defined structure, making it challenging for some teams to manage. The focus on short-term tasks may make it less suitable for projects requiring extensive long-term planning.

---

made, systems running the Kanban Toyota strategy will have only as many as are needed for a specific amount of time.

[51] Microsoft Teams Integration - Visual Studio Marketplace - Developers and product managers can track and create new work items by bringing their VSTS Kanban boards right into Microsoft Teams. All your favourite Kanban board features - live refresh, card styling, tag colouring, extensions, and more - are available without leaving your team's channel.

Other Project Management Methodologies

The good news is that Waterfall, Agile and Kanban are not your only picks. You can also choose between any of the following nine popular frameworks. These are:

- *Scrum methodology* which involves short "sprints" that are used to create a project cycle,
- *Scrumban* which is a methodology that draws inspiration from both Scrum and Kanban frameworks,
- *PRINCE2* otherwise known as **PR**ojects **IN** **C**ontrolled **E**nvironments, uses the overarching waterfall methodology to define stages within a project,
- *Lean* aims to cut waste and create a simple framework for project needs,
- *Six Sigma* which is used for quality management and is frequently described as a philosophy rather than a traditional methodology e.g. lean Six Sigma or Agile Six Sigma;
- *Critical path method (CPM)* which works to identify and schedule critical tasks within a project – work breakdown structure,
- *Critical chain project management (CCPM)* is closely related to the critical path methodology but is even more detailed, making it one of the most comprehensive options
- *Extreme programming (XP)* which used for fast-paced projects with tight deadlines, or
- *Project Management Institute's (PMBOK®)* Guide

Over the years, I have observed how BI teams work together and collaborate to deliver analytical projects. Based on my experience, I have identified some considerations that BI teams can take into account. These will help answer questions like "What should every analyst manager and team leader know about leadership?" and "What qualities make a good BI manager?"

LEADERSHIP TRUTHS EVERY ANALYST MANAGER AND TEAM LEADER SHOULD EMBRACE

As we progress in our careers, we are often taught that managing teams is the ultimate goal. However, when it comes to leading a team in the field of data analysis, it takes more than just technical expertise. Effective leadership also involves understanding how to manage teams and cultivate a positive work environment. While we may follow project management methodologies, it's important to ensure they're implemented correctly to achieve the desired outcome.

In order to achieve the desired outcome, there are questions managers might be asking. Not being able to address these questions appropriately might lead to imposter syndrome. Imposter syndrome is common among BI managers due to the fast-paced nature of data and BI analysis. While questions might be asked in many ways, you might find answers as we address: (1) What happens when your best analysts leave, (2) How to build trust in a remote workplace, (3) Managing feedback, (4) How your values could build trust through your actions, (5) How to embrace Diversity, Equity, and Inclusion (DEI), and (6) How to negotiate employee salaries.

When Your Best People Leave, It's Not Them - It's You

We have been accustomed to this common phrase that implies the reason why analysts leave a company is not because of their personal circumstances, but because of the team's culture, company policies, top management (Exco/Manco), or work environment. We as analyst managers are responsible for their departure. The BI analyst is responsible for creating a positive and engaging workplace that retains talent and prevents turnover. Some of the factors that can influence analyst retention are:

- Competitive and fair compensation;
- Recognition and appreciation;
- Career development and advancement opportunities;
- Flexible work arrangements and work-life balance;
- Clear and frequent communication and feedback;
- Trust and respect;
- Employee engagement and involvement; and
- Organisational values and mission.

Recognising why high-performing team members leave could be linked to leadership and organisational issues. It is the first step towards improvement. Addressing these issues can lead to better retention and a more positive work atmosphere. Failing to acknowledge this truth can perpetuate a cycle of talent loss, impacting team morale and overall productivity. Let us imagine a tech company that lost its top data scientist to a competitor offering similar compensation. However, upon closer inspection, the scientist cited a lack of career growth and minimal recognition for contributions as the primary reasons for leaving. Sometimes we might lose team members to another team within the department or to another department within the organisation. What is important is the ability to recognise what drives the migration of top talent.

If we continue to refuse to acknowledge our role in employee departures, we might start to experience diminishing morale, decreased innovation, and higher staff turnover rates. We know that these are Key Performance Indicators (KPIs) that measure the effectiveness of our leadership. I would suggest that we engage in regular one-on-one conversations to understand employee concerns, provide growth opportunities, and create an environment where achievements are acknowledged and rewarded. We might even start to ask "How could we appropriately manage remote teams?"

You Don't Have A Remote Work Issue - You Have Trust Issues

The word "appropriately manage" implies that the main challenge we don't allow our BI teams to remote work is not the technical or logistical aspects, but the psychological and relational ones. The phrase suggests that the root cause of many remote work problems is the lack of trust between managers and employees, or among team members. Trust is essential for effective collaboration, communication, innovation, and performance in any work setting, but especially in a remote one, where there are fewer opportunities to observe and interact with each other. Building trust with remote teams fosters a sense of autonomy, leading to enhanced productivity and work-life balance.

On the other side, micromanaging remote workers due to distrust can stifle creativity, hinder productivity, and strain relationships. Some of the signs that indicate trust issues in a remote workplace are micromanaging or over-monitoring employees' activities and outputs, communicating poorly or inconsistently, failing to recognize or appreciate employees' contributions, avoiding feedback or conflict resolution, withholding information or resources, blaming, or criticising others for mistakes or failures, and excluding or isolating some team members.

A data analysis team that shifted to remote work during the pandemic might experience similar issues. The manager's initial inclination to track hours and tasks could result in decreased output and a sense of resentment among the team. We all remember how productivity increased during the hard lockdown of the COVID-19 pandemic. What happened to reduce productivity and increase staff turnover? Teams marred by distrust might experience communication breakdowns, decreased collaboration, and attrition. I further believe that the solution is to focus on outcomes rather than processes. Let us set clear expectations, encourage open communication, and leverage technology for seamless collaboration. Open communication implies that we need to embrace all kinds of feedback. You might be asking "Will a team survive if we don't embrace feedback?"

Management That Can't Handle Feedback Won't Survive Change

Analyst managers who are not open to receiving and acting on employee feedback are likely to fail in leading and implementing change initiatives in their organisations. Most organisations send middle managers for development courses in business schools to learn how to receive feedback. We know that analyst feedback is a valuable source of information that can help us understand how our BI teams are experiencing and responding to change, as well as identify any barriers or gaps that need to be addressed. Managers who can't handle feedback may be resistant to change themselves or may lack the skills or confidence to communicate and engage with their employees effectively during change.

We don't want to be managers against feedback as we may also miss the opportunity to build trust and rapport with our analyst teams, which are essential for creating a positive and supportive work culture that embraces change. Other negative consequences they may face are lower team engagement, higher turnover, lower productivity, lower quality, lower customer satisfaction, and higher costs.

Yes, all the above points could be unlocked by knowing how to receive feedback.

Therefore, managers who want to survive and succeed in change need to learn how to solicit, listen, and act on employee feedback in a constructive and respectful way. Doing so can help them create more effective and sustainable change outcomes for their organisations. Embracing feedback cultivates a culture of continuous improvement and adaptability, crucial in today's dynamic business landscape.

Rejecting feedback can lead to a stagnant team, and resistance to change, innovation, and growth. Let's think about a BI team that struggled to adapt to new reporting tools due to the manager's resistance to suggestions. This may hinder the team's ability to streamline processes and provide accurate insights. The fate of this team is that it might become obsolete in rapidly evolving industries. To avoid this, let us create an environment where constructive criticism is valued, and encourage open discussions about processes, tools, and strategies. I hope by now you can see the importance of showing our teams that we value their feedback.

If Your Actions Don't Align With Your Values, Your Team Won't Trust You

Leaders need to act in accordance with their stated values, or else they will lose the trust and respect of their employees. Values are the principles and beliefs that guide a leader's decisions and actions. They reflect what the leader cares about and stands for. Leading by example and demonstrating alignment between words and actions enhances credibility and builds strong employee-manager relationships. The disadvantage is that a misalignment between stated values and actions can lead to cynicism, distrust, and reduced commitment from team members.

Imagine an analytics start-up that claimed to prioritise work-life balance but frequently required employees to work long hours without proper compensation or flexibility. Wouldn't you feel like work-life balance is just lip service? We have the same issue of diversity and inclusion here in South Africa. We hear top management speak about inclusion and regularly witness the exclusion of non-managerial staff in strategic offsites. The danger is that teams led by managers whose actions contradict their professed values might experience decreased engagement, higher turnover, and difficulty in attracting top talent. To curb this,

I would suggest that we live the values we promote. Let us prioritize work-life balance, ethical decision-making, and transparency in actions and decisions.

Your Diversity Program Is Hollow If Your Leadership Team All Looks The Same

This could have a negative impact on all analyst team managers, especially if it reflects the reality of their organisation. It could imply that managers are not committed to promoting Diversity, Equity, and Inclusion (DEI) in their team or in the company. It could also suggest that the team leaders are not aware of the benefits of having a diverse and inclusive leadership team, such as improved decision-making, innovation, performance, and customer satisfaction. If you are an analyst manager who didn't know, a diverse team brings varied perspectives and innovative solutions, which positively influence team dynamics and decision-making. You might be able to complete projects on time and so forth.

The lack of diversity in leadership perpetuates inequality, limits creativity, and inhibits understanding of diverse customer bases. An analytics company that had an impressive diversity recruitment program but an all-male leadership team sends a different message. The incongruence could result in a perception of tokenism and thus hinder the company's commitment to inclusion. Analyst teams with this type of "homogeneous leadership" might struggle to attract diverse talent, leading to limited growth and a stagnant work culture. Very few of us would want to work in an organisation where we feel like an outsider, or where they would feel that the seats are not reserved for someone like them. I have seen my team choose an outsider over me and I left within three months of joining the team. This is despite my almost two decades tenure with the organisation. I strongly believe that we need to prioritise DEI at all levels, actively seeking underrepresented talent for leadership roles, and creating an inclusive environment. Especially being transparent as managers about fair pay for our DEI candidates.

Underpaying Your People Doesn't Make You Cost-Effective - It Makes You Short-Sighted

If you think you read the title incorrectly remember that I don't work at the bank anymore. I didn't know that I was underpaid until I went to two interviews and was told I didn't make the cut, even though I was the best, due to my low salary. My experience will allow you to see that underpaying employees can have negative consequences for the company in the long term, such as:

- *Lower employee retention*: Underpaid Employees are more likely to leave the company for better opportunities elsewhere thus resulting in high turnover rates. They can be costly and disruptive for the company. According to a study by Harvard University, a $1 per hour pay increase among warehouse workers resulted in a 2.8% increase in retention. Conversely, every $1 per hour loss in pay resulted in a 28% increase in turnover rates[52].
- *Lower employee performance*: Employees who are underpaid may feel demotivated, dissatisfied, or resentful towards their employer. This can affect their productivity,

[52] Emanuel N & Harrington E, The payoffs of higher pay: elasticities of productivity and labor supply with respect to wages, emanuel_jmp.pdf (harvard.edu)

quality, and creativity at work. They may also be less willing to go the extra mile, take initiative, or collaborate with others. A study by Glassdoor found that a 10% higher base pay is associated with a 1.5% increase in employee satisfaction, which can translate into higher performance[53].

- *Lower employee loyalty*: Employees who are underpaid may not trust or respect their employer or feel valued or appreciated by them. This can erode their commitment and engagement with the company's vision, mission, and goals. They may also be more likely to speak negatively about the company to others or to act unethically or dishonestly. A study by PwC[54] found that 59% of employees said that being paid is one of the most important attributes of an employer.

Given the above research, we can now see how fair compensation leads to higher motivation, increased loyalty, and improved performance, ultimately benefiting the organisation's bottom line. Teams that prioritize short-term cost savings over fair compensation may find themselves grappling with constant turnover, low morale, and decreased overall productivity. Let us

[53] Why Do Workers Quit? The Factors That Predict Employee Turnover - Glassdoor Economic Research - Pay also matters for employee turnover. We find that a 10 percent increase in base pay raises the likelihood by 1.5 percent that the average employee will stay inside the company when moving to their next role, even after statistically controlling for factors like job title, industry, company size and location.

[54] Future of work: PwC - Companies on hiring sprees are refining employee value propositions, focusing above all on corporate purpose and leadership. While those are important, they should expect candidates to negotiate hard for what they now see as table stakes: competitive packages and perks coupled with flexibility and expanded benefits such as career growth and upskilling opportunities. Some may also see job changes as an opportunity to close pay gaps. Women are more likely than men to be seeking higher salaries (46% versus 34%). And more Hispanic and Black employees are looking (82% and 67%, respectively) compared to white/non-Hispanics (57%).

be fair in our dealings. Being transparent won't make us weaker but will strengthen trust between us and the entire team. Let us conduct regular salary benchmarking, ensure compensation is competitive, and offer opportunities for growth and advancement.

KEY TAKEAWAYS

In this chapter, we have explored the different roles and responsibilities within a Business Intelligence (BI) team. As BI becomes more critical for organisations to make informed decisions, various roles have emerged to handle different aspects of data analysis, data modelling, and data visualization.

- **Data Engineer**: The role of a data engineer is to source, organize, and move data between systems. They are responsible for data storage and infrastructure decisions. Key competencies of data engineers include:
    - *Extract, Transform, and Load (ETL):* They automate data feeds or migrate data from various systems, ensuring data quality and consistency.
    - *Data Warehouse (DW) Creation:* Data engineers design and implement data warehouses to store all the data needed for business analysis in one place.
    - *Data Governance:* Data engineers focus on ensuring data security and integrity.
    - *Data System Knowledge:* They must understand data structures and other ways to help analysts avoid data issues.

Data engineers work with various types of database systems, such as Online Transaction Processing (OLTP), Data Lake, Data

Warehouse (DW), and Data Mart, to optimize data storage and access.

- **Data Analyst**: Data analysts are responsible for building data models and metrics that facilitate analysis and visualization. Their main responsibilities include:
    - *ETL:* Like data engineers, data analysts import and transform data into the desired format for analysis.
    - *Calculating Metrics:* Data analysts use formulas to calculate business performance metrics.
    - *Creating Data Models:* They combine tables and link related data to create data models that refresh automatically.
    - *Documentation:* Data analysts document data models and metric definitions for other analysts to use.

Data analysts often use tools like Microsoft Excel, VBA, Access, Power Query, Tableau, Power Pivot, or Power BI for their analysis work.

- **Data Visualization Specialist**: Data visualization specialists focus on turning clean data into visuals that communicate insights effectively. Their key responsibilities include:
    - *Creating Data Visuals:* They design visuals that highlight key data points and trends.

- *Building Dashboards:* Data visualization specialists combine multiple visuals into dashboards that tell a story using data.
- *Communicating Results:* They present findings to management meetings and manage audience permissions.
- *Feedback and Improvement:* Data visualization specialists gather feedback from the audience to improve report clarity and definitions.

These specialists often work with tools like Tableau, Power BI, Excel, MicroStrategy, Qlik, Looker, Sisense, Dundas BI, Python, Adaptive Insights, Plotly, or other analytical tools.

- **Business Intelligence Team/Department**: A typical BI team consists of data engineers, data analysts, data visualization specialists, and team leaders or senior managers who assist with decision-making. The team is organized into squads, with each squad focused on specific data domains or business functions. Data engineers ensure data is sourced and prepared for analysis, data analysts build data models and metrics, and data visualization specialists create visuals and dashboards to communicate insights effectively. The entire BI team works in alignment with the organisation's management committee (Manco) to guide data and analysis strategy and enable better decision-making.

Understanding the roles and responsibilities within a BI team is essential for organisations seeking to leverage data-driven insights. BI plays a crucial role in providing actionable insights to senior management and business leaders, helping them make informed decisions to maintain or change their course of action. As the demand for BI continues to grow, having specialized roles within the team enables a more focused and efficient approach to data analysis and visualization. The relationship between the BI team and the management committee is crucial in driving the organisation's success through data-driven decision-making.

BI team management is a dynamic and challenging field that requires a combination of technical skills, interpersonal skills, and leadership skills. We need to be able to communicate effectively with different stakeholders, coordinate and motivate their team members, monitor, and control the data analysis project's progress, and deliver value to their customers. Being a BI manager can be rewarding and fulfilling, as it allows us to make a positive impact on their organisation and society. Choosing the right methodology depends on the project's nature, requirements, and team dynamics. Waterfall, Agile, and Kanban offer distinct approaches to team management, each with its strengths and weaknesses. By understanding these methodologies and their real-life success stories, we as managers can make informed decisions to deliver successful outcomes and become effective leaders.

Becoming an effective leader in BI analysis requires us to embrace the six leadership truths. It's not just about technical skills, but also about mastering these signposts on the path to success. By exploring these truths, understanding their dimensions, and enacting strategies to overcome their challenges, we can embark on a transformative journey that shapes not only our leadership but also the trajectory of our teams. It's important to remember that leadership is a continual evolution, and each truth serves as a beacon of growth and progress. To cultivate thriving teams that drive innovation, growth, and success, we need to understand the advantages and disadvantages of each truth, learn from real-life examples, anticipate potential outcomes, and implement strategic solutions. Let's walk this path together and strive towards leadership excellence.

chapter 6

UNDERSTANDING DATA STRUCTURES AND DATA RELATIONSHIPS

It's quite amazing how computers store data. I used to think that data could only be stored on hard drives (HDDs). During my honours in Informatics at University I finally understood how much it means to know data structures. Data structures are fundamental concepts in computer science and play a crucial role in data analysis. Back in the 2010s when I was a novice analyst, I didn't know that understanding different data structures would empower me to organize and manipulate data effectively. It was only in 2016 that I understood this fact.

In this chapter, we will explore several important data structures: (1) variables, (2) data tables, (3) lists, arrays, (4) key-value pairs, and (5) hash tables. I know this sounds a little goofy and I assure you that you will be blown away at the end of this chapter. So let me not waste more time, Let's dive in!

WHAT ARE VARIABLES?

Variables are the building blocks of data manipulation. I call them building blocks because they represent a storage location that can hold a value or data. This is the foundation of data analysis. In data analysis, variables can store different types of information, such as numbers, text, dates, or Boolean values. I was taught to declare variables when coding to ensure that a certain value gets stored in a form. It's like playing the broken telephone game and using variables to ensure the same remains the same. They provide a way to reference and modify data throughout your analysis (broken telephone game). By assigning appropriate names to variables, you can easily identify and work with specific pieces of data. It is like remembering who said what at a dinner party instead of remembering the general conversation.

WHY ARE DATA TABLES COMMON?

Data tables, also known as datasets, are a structured way to store and organize data. This data structure consists of rows and columns. Each represents a record or observation, and each represents a specific attribute or variable. It is like opening an Excel spreadsheet and seeing the empty cells as variables stored in rows and columns. Data tables provide a tabular format that allows for efficient data manipulation, filtering, sorting, and analysis. Popular tools for working with data tables include spreadsheet software like Microsoft Excel and Google Sheets. I'm sure you would understand why this is a common data structure. I however love datasets that are stored in databases accessible using SQL language.

ARE LISTS SYNONYMOUS WITH TABLES?

A list is an ordered collection of elements or items. Unlike data tables, lists are typically one-dimensional and can contain elements of different data types. For example, a list of numbers, a list of names, or a list of mixed data types. This is like looking at only one column of your Excel or Google sheet. Why would I choose Lists instead of tables? It is because Lists are flexible and allow for dynamic resizing, making them suitable for scenarios where the number of elements may change over time. As a novice analyst, I often used lists to perform iterative operations or store data sequentially.

WHAT ABOUT CREATING ARRAYS?

Arrays are like lists as they also store collections of elements or variables. However, arrays have a fixed size (not dynamic in size) and hold elements of the same data type. This fixed size provides efficient access and manipulation of elements within the array. Arrays are widely used in data analysis and programming languages to store large volumes of similar data. I used to use arrays to store answers to questions which will be saved when you complete the questionnaire. It allows for data to be stored on temporary memory (RAM) before it gets committed to an HDD. Arrays offer fast retrieval, because they are stored on RAM and not HDD, and are especially useful for numerical computations and algorithms.

DO WE NEED KEY-VALUE PAIRS?

Key-value pairs represent a data structure that associates a unique key with a corresponding value. Keys act as identifiers and provide a way to access and retrieve specific values from the data structure. I have often used this in my analysis which is magical when you link data tables. This is because Key-value pairs are often used in scenarios where we need fast data retrieval such as dictionaries or lookup tables. To understand this better, think of an instance when you use a person's name (key) to retrieve their corresponding contact information (value) in an address book.

WHAT'S THE IMPORTANCE OF HASH TABLES?

I'm assuming that you were asking yourself where the Kay-value pair reference table gets stored. Are they being stored as a list, table, or array? This is where hash tables come to light. Hash tables, also known as hash maps, are a type of data structure that provides efficient insertion, deletion, and retrieval of key-value pairs. The best Hash Table is the one storing the directory to all data in your HDD. Yes, when you format your HDD, you don't delete anything in the HDD itself but rather delete the Hash Table. The data is still there. I was taught to recover the data in the Computer Forensic module. Hash Tables utilise a hashing function to map keys to an index or position within an underlying array. This mapping allows for fast access to values based on their keys. Hash tables are widely used in various applications, such as caching, indexing, and implementing associative arrays.

UNDERSTANDING THE TYPES OF RELATIONSHIPS IN DATA

Have you battled with duplicates in your data table? Are you taking valuable time analysing tables separately? As the adage goes, "Knowledge is power". This sentiment rings particularly true when dealing with data. The diverse forms of relationships between data sets enable us to better understand, manage, and manipulate information to derive useful insights. However, the reality of duplicates in data complicates these relationships and can skew the conclusions derived.

Establishing relationships between datasets can help to alleviate data duplication, ensure consistency, and improve the overall management of information. The core types of relationships are "Many to One", "One to One", and "Many to Many". Each type carries a distinct structure and function which serves to maintain data integrity and streamline data operations. Let us waste no time and explore the concepts of Many to One, One to One, and Many to Many relationships, and how they aid in understanding and managing duplicate values in data.

Many-to-One Relationships

A Many-to-One relationship in data implies that a key may appear multiple times in one table but only once in another. Essentially, this means a single record from one table is associated with multiple records from another. Consider an example where we have two tables – 'Authors' and 'Books'. The 'Authors' table has unique entries for each author, while the 'Books' table has entries for every book, including multiple books written by the same author. This is a classic Many-to-one relationship, where multiple books (many) correspond to a single author (one).

This type of relationship is crucial in identifying duplicate data, especially in the table where the key appears multiple times. It can help single out duplicate entries that do not correlate with a unique record in the related table, flagging potential inconsistencies and inaccuracies in data. With this understanding, data administrators can then decide whether duplicates are appropriate or require management and resolution.

One-to-One Relationships

A One-to-one relationship represents a scenario where each key appears only once in each table. Each entry in one table corresponds uniquely and exclusively to a single entry in another table. For instance, let's consider two tables – 'Employees' and 'Employee_IDs'. Each employee has a unique ID, and each ID is associated with a specific employee. Hence, there's a one-to-one correspondence between the records in both tables. One-to-one relationships offer an easy means of managing duplicates because each entry should only appear once in each table. Any duplication of keys is immediately identifiable as an error. These relationships maintain data integrity and enable accurate linkages between tables, making data management simpler and more efficient.

Many to Many Relationships (Avoid Where Possible)

Many-to-many relationships signify that each key may appear multiple times in both tables. This type of relationship can often lead to data complexity and redundancy. To illustrate, imagine two tables – 'Students' and 'Courses'. A student can enrol in multiple courses, and a course can be taken by multiple students. This creates a Many-to-Many relationship, where multiple courses (many) are associated with multiple students (many).

While Many-to-Many relationships offer flexibility in data organisation, they are often challenging to manage due to the high possibility of duplicate entries in both tables. They often necessitate a "link" or "junction" table to prevent data redundancy and preserve the overall integrity of the data.

DEMYSTIFYING DATABASE TYPES

Have you recently asked yourself about database types? If not, did you know that in the world of data management, databases play a pivotal role in storing, organizing, and retrieving information? Knowing about databases could be useful for us especially now that we know how data is stored in HDDs. Novice analysts often encounter a wide array of database types, each tailored to specific use cases. We may battle to understand why one database type was chosen instead of another. I aim to shed light on some of the most common database types, their characteristics, advantages, disadvantages, and the ideal scenarios for their implementation. We will be discussing:

- Relational Databases,
- Document Databases,
- Graph Databases,
- Analytical Databases,
- Column-Family databases, and
- Key-Value databases.

While we discuss the above, please be cognisant that SQL (Structured Query Language) and NoSQL (Not Only SQL) are two contrasting approaches to database management[55]. Each of the two has its own strengths and weaknesses. Upon research, we will realise that the choice between SQL and NoSQL depends on our specific project requirements. SQL databases offer strong data integrity and well-defined data structures, while NoSQL databases provide flexibility, scalability, and adaptability to various data models and use cases. It's essential to evaluate the strengths and weaknesses of each approach based on your application's needs. I believe that knowing much more about each will make us choose better to improve our analysis.

Relational Database (SQL)

A Relational Database, often referred to as an SQL (Structured Query Language) database, is a type of database that organises and stores data in structured tables with predefined schemas. Did you know that it is based on the principles of the relational model,

[55] Know the Difference: SQL (Structured Query Language) and NoSQL (Not Only SQL) – Being an Analyst Blog - This article shows a comparison of the two using (1) Data Model, (2) Schema, (3) Query language, (4) Data Relationships, (5) Scalability, (6) Consistency and ACID, and (7) Use Cases.

which was introduced by E.F. Codd in 1970[56]? If not, now you know. Besides, in a relational database, data is organised into rows and columns, where each row represents a record, and each column represents an attribute or field of that record. The relationships between records are established through keys, typically primary keys and foreign keys. Key characteristics of Relational Databases include:

- *Structured Data* - Data is stored in well-defined tables with specific data types for each column, ensuring consistency and organisation,
- *Schema* - A relational database enforces a fixed schema that specifies the structure of the data and the relationships between tables.
- *ACID Compliance* - ACID stands for Atomicity, Consistency, Isolation, and Durability. These properties ensure that transactions are reliably processed, even in the face of failures.
- *Data Integrity* - Relational databases maintain data integrity by enforcing constraints such as uniqueness, primary keys, foreign keys, and data types.
- *SQL Queries* - Data manipulation and querying are performed using SQL, a standardized language for

---

[56] All about Relational Database Models | Smartsheet - The relational model was developed by E. F. Codd, who drew on a variety of mathematical theories, including Claude Shannon's informational theory from 1948, as well as set theory dating back to the late 1800s. Codd's own contributions to the field, such as relational algebra and relational calculus, were also instrumental in the development of this model. Codd recognized that using attribute names instead of data ordering would be more effective in a relational database. He formulated 12 rules for this model, among which the information principle stands out: all information in a relational database should be represented explicitly in tables at the logical level. To improve response time for relational algebra queries, developers can employ algebraic laws to convert them into faster-processing equivalents.

managing relational databases. SQL allows users to create, retrieve, update, and delete data.

The advantages of Relational Databases Include and are not limited to:

- *Mature Technology* - Relational databases have been in use for decades, resulting in a wealth of resources, tools, and expertise;
- *Data integrity* - Enforces data consistency through predefined relationships; and
- *Data Relationships* - They are well-suited for applications with complex data relationships that require joins and relational operations.

Contrary to the wonderful advantages are the disadvantages of relational databases which include:

- *Scalability Challenges* - Traditional relational databases can face challenges when scaling to handle extremely large datasets or high-velocity data;
- *Schema Changes* - Modifying the schema of a relational database can be complex and require careful planning to avoid disruptions;
- *Performance* - For certain types of queries and workloads, relational databases might not offer the same performance as some NoSQL databases optimized for specific use cases.

We can see from the above how the ideal place for relational databases is for scenarios that require well-defined data structures, strong data integrity, complex data relationships, and ACID compliance. I have been introduced to these databases during my tenure at the bank. This is because they are commonly used in applications like financial systems, Customer Relationship Management (CRM) systems, Enterprise Resource Planning (ERP) systems, and situations where data consistency and reliability are paramount.

Document Database (NoSQL)

A Document Database is a type of NoSQL (Not Only SQL) database that stores and manages data in a format like documents. Instead of using tables with fixed schemas like relational databases, document databases store data as flexible and self-contained documents, often in formats like JSON (JavaScript Object Notation) or BSON (Binary JSON). Each document can have varying structures and attributes, allowing for more flexibility in data representation compared to traditional relational databases. Key characteristics of Document Databases include:

- *Flexible Schema* - Document databases do not require a fixed schema. Each document can have its structure, and fields can be added or removed as needed without affecting other documents.
- *No Joins* - Unlike relational databases, document databases typically avoid complex joins by storing related data within a single document or through references.

- *Scalability* - Many document databases are designed for horizontal scalability, allowing them to distribute data across multiple servers to handle large datasets and high-velocity data.
- *Semi-Structured Data* - Document databases are suitable for storing semi-structured or unstructured data, making them well-suited for applications with evolving data requirements.
- *API-Based Queries* - Document databases often provide API-based querying mechanisms for retrieving and manipulating data.

Advantages of Document Databases include:

- *Schema Flexibility* - Document databases accommodate changing data structures without requiring changes to the entire database schema;
- *Performance* - Due to their self-contained nature, documents can be retrieved with a single query, leading to efficient data retrieval;
- *Variety of Data* - They are suitable for applications with varied data types, formats, and structures.

The disadvantages of Document Databases include:

- *Complex Queries* - Some advanced queries involving multiple documents might require application-level logic, as document databases are not optimised for complex joins;

- *Data Consistency* - Ensuring consistency across documents with relationships can be challenging, especially in distributed setups;
- *ACID Transactions* - While some document databases support transactions, they might not provide the same level of ACID compliance as relational databases.

Document databases are particularly well-suited for scenarios where data structures are not fixed, and the application requires the ability to evolve its data model over time. They are commonly used in content management systems, e-commerce platforms, blogging platforms, and applications where unstructured or semi-structured data needs to be stored and retrieved efficiently. If your project involves rapid development, frequent schema changes, and a need for flexible data representation, a document database might be a suitable choice.

Graph Database (NoSQL)

A Graph Database is a type of NoSQL database designed to store and manage data in the form of nodes and edges, representing entities and their relationships. Graph databases are specifically optimised for exploring and traversing complex relationships between data points. They excel at answering questions about how entities are connected and understanding patterns within intricate networks. Key characteristics of Graph Databases include:

- *Graph Structure* - Data is stored as nodes (entities) and edges (relationships) connecting these nodes. Each node and edge can have properties that provide additional information.

- *Relationship Focus* - Graph databases prioritize relationships, allowing efficient querying and traversal of connections between entities.
- *Graph Algorithms* - Graph databases often come with built-in graph algorithms that can be used to analyse and discover patterns within the data.
- *Schema Flexibility* - While some graph databases allow for predefined schemas, many provide flexibility in adding new nodes and relationships without altering the entire structure.
- *Complex Queries* - Graph databases excel in answering complex queries involving multiple levels of relationships.

The advantages of using Graph Databases include:

- *Relationship Analysis* - Graph databases excel at revealing hidden relationships and patterns within data, making them ideal for applications that require understanding connections;
- *Flexible Queries* - Graph databases allow for complex, recursive, and pattern-based queries that can uncover insights that might be difficult to discover in other database types;
- *Performance* - For scenarios that involve analysing relationships, graph databases can outperform relational databases due to their optimised data structure.

Well, not all is great with Graph Databases, here are some disadvantages:

- *Performance Complexity* - Extremely large graphs with many relationships can lead to performance challenges, requiring careful consideration of indexing and optimisation strategies; and
- *Data Complexity* - While powerful, graph databases might not be the best fit for all data types or applications, especially those that don't heavily rely on relationships.

Graph databases are most appropriate for scenarios where understanding relationships and connections between data points is essential. They shine in applications like social networks, recommendation systems, fraud detection, network analysis, and knowledge graphs. If your project involves intricate data relationships and the ability to quickly traverse and analyse these connections, a graph database might be a valuable choice to uncover insights that other database types might miss.

Analytical Database (OLAP/SQL)

An Analytical Database, often referred to as an OLAP (Online Analytical Processing) database, is a type of database specifically designed for complex data analysis and reporting. We used to refer to it as a “cube” because of legacy software. Unlike transactional databases that focus on capturing and processing real-time transactions, analytical databases are optimised for querying and aggregating large volumes of historical data to support business intelligence and decision-making processes. They store historical data and enable multidimensional analysis.

Key characteristics of Analytical Databases include:

- *Multidimensional Data Model* - Analytical databases use a multidimensional data model, which involves organising data into dimensions and measures. Dimensions represent attributes that describe the data, while measures are numeric values that can be aggregated (e.g., sales revenue),
- *Aggregation and Summarisation* - Analytical databases excel at aggregating and summarizing data to generate reports, dashboards, and visualizations. They allow users to perform calculations across various dimensions and hierarchies;
- *Complex Queries* - Analytical databases support complex queries involving multiple dimensions, measures, and levels of aggregation. These queries help extract insights and patterns from historical data;
- *Historical Data* - Analytical databases store historical data, making them suitable for trend analysis, historical comparisons, and identifying long-term patterns;
- *Data Warehousing* - Analytical databases are often used in data warehousing environments, where data from different sources is integrated, transformed, and loaded for analysis.

The advantages of Analytical Databases over other types include:

- *High Performance* - Analytical databases are optimized for complex querying and aggregation, enabling fast response times for analytical queries;

- *Aggregation Capabilities* - These databases provide built-in capabilities for summarising and aggregating data, making it easier to generate reports and perform analysis;
- *Business Intelligence* - Analytical databases serve as a foundation for business intelligence tools, enabling users to gain insights into historical data and make informed decisions. I know that Power BI and Power Query encourage us to use OLAP connections for analysis;
- *Large-Scale Data Analysis* - They can handle large datasets, making them suitable for organisations with substantial amounts of historical data.

As much as I love working with OLAP/"cube" data there are a few disadvantages of using Analytical Databases which include:

- *Data Freshness* - Analytical databases may not provide real-time data updates, as they are typically loaded with batch processes and focus on historical data;
- *Complex Setup* - Designing, setting up, and maintaining an analytical database can be complex, requiring specialised skills;
- *Limited Transactional Support* - Analytical databases are optimised for querying and analysis, but they might not offer the same level of transactional support as traditional relational databases.

Analytical databases are suitable for scenarios where historical data analysis, complex querying, and reporting are crucial. They are commonly used in business intelligence, data warehousing, and decision support systems. If your project involves generating reports, conducting trend analysis, or performing multidimensional data exploration, an analytical database can provide the necessary tools and capabilities to derive insights from large volumes of historical data.

Column-Family Database (NoSQL)

A Column-Family Database is a type of NoSQL database that stores and manages data in column families, providing an alternative data model to traditional row-based databases. This database type is particularly well-suited for handling large amounts of data while optimising read operations for specific columns or attributes.

Key characteristics of column-family databases include:

- *Columnar Storage* - Unlike traditional row-based databases, column-family databases store data in columns rather than rows. Data for each column is stored together, allowing for more efficient read operations when only specific columns need to be retrieved;
- *Distributed Architecture* - Many column-family databases are designed for horizontal scalability, meaning they can distribute data across multiple servers to handle large datasets and high-velocity data;
- *Scalability and Performance* - Column-family databases are optimized for read-intensive and write-heavy workloads, making them suitable for scenarios with frequent queries and aggregations;

- *Schema Flexibility* - Some column-family databases provide flexibility in terms of column addition and deletion, allowing data models to evolve;
- *Compression and Encoding* - Due to their columnar storage, these databases can implement compression and encoding techniques that reduce storage requirements and improve query performance.

I know we are not accustomed to querying columns but here are a few advantages of using Column-Family databases:

- *Efficient Read Operations* - Retrieving specific columns is highly efficient due to the column-oriented storage, making them suitable for analytics and reporting;
- *Scalability* - Many column-family databases can scale horizontally, distributing data across multiple nodes to handle large datasets;
- *Compression and Storage Efficiency* - Column-family databases can often achieve high levels of compression, resulting in reduced storage costs;
- *Analytics and Aggregation* - They excel in scenarios that involve analytical queries and aggregations on specific columns.

But, as you would have guessed, Column-Family Databases come with their own disadvantages. Here are some disadvantages:

- *Complex Queries* - Queries that require data across multiple column families or complex joins can be challenging to formulate and execute;
- *Limited Transactional Support* - Some column-family databases prioritize read performance over transactional consistency, which might not be suitable for all use cases; and
- *Data Relationships* - While column-family databases can handle relationships to some extent, they might not be as optimized for relationship management as other database types.

Column-family databases are well-suited for scenarios that involve time-series data, logging systems, real-time analytics, and applications where read performance and scalability are critical. They are often chosen when optimising for column-oriented queries, aggregation of specific attributes, and scenarios where data is write-intensive and read-heavy. If your project involves scenarios where data needs to be quickly aggregated and analysed based on specific attributes or columns, a column-family database might be a suitable choice.

Key-Value Database (NoSQL)

A Key-Value Database is a type of NoSQL database that stores and retrieves data using a simple key-value pair model. In this model, each piece of data (value) is associated with a unique identifier (key), allowing for efficient and quick data retrieval. Key-value databases prioritise speed and simplicity, making them well-suited for scenarios where rapid data access is crucial. Key characteristics of key-value databases include:

- *Simplicity* - Key-value databases have a straightforward data model, with each piece of data being stored and retrieved using a single key.
- *High Performance* - These databases are optimised for quick read and write operations, making them ideal for use cases that require rapid data access.
- *Schema Flexibility* - Key-value databases typically do not enforce a strict schema, allowing for the storage of varying data structures without affecting the entire database.
- *Scalability* - Many key-value databases are designed for horizontal scalability, distributing data across multiple servers to handle growing datasets and traffic.
- *Caching* - Key-value databases are commonly used for caching frequently accessed data, improving application performance by reducing the need to fetch data from slower storage layers.

The advantages of Key-Value Databases include:

- *Speed* - The simplicity of the key-value model allows for lightning-fast read and write operations;
- *Scalability* - Many key-value databases are built to scale horizontally, enabling them to handle increased data loads;
- *Flexible Data* - They accommodate various data types and structures, making them versatile for different use cases.

The other side of Key-Value Databases includes:

- *Limited Querying* - Key-value databases are not well-suited for complex queries and aggregations that involve multiple keys or values;

- *Lack of Relationships* - While some key-value databases offer limited support for relationships, they are not designed for complex data relationships;
- *Data Consistency* - Maintaining consistency across different key-value pairs can be challenging, especially in distributed setups.

Key-value databases are ideal for scenarios that prioritize quick data access, caching, and situations where data is best represented as individual pieces of information associated with unique keys. They are commonly used for applications like session management, caching, real-time analytics, and scenarios where fast read and write operations are essential. If your project requires rapid data retrieval, simple data structures, and efficient caching mechanisms, a key-value database might be a suitable choice.

ROLE OF STRUCTURES IN DATA ANALYSIS

In computer science, data structures are vital concepts that play a crucial role in data analysis. They are essential tools for any analyst working with data and offer different ways to effectively organize and manipulate data. These include variables, data tables, lists, arrays, key-value pairs, and hash tables. By understanding these fundamental data structures, one can develop the necessary skills to tackle complex data analysis tasks and build efficient algorithms. We can broaden our understanding while discussing (1) Relational Databases, (2) Document Databases, (3) Graph Databases, (4) Analytical Databases, (5) Column-Family databases, and (6) Key-Value databases.

I have mentioned how I realised the importance of knowing data structures and distinguishing between database types during my Informatics honours at University. My suggestion is that we continue to explore and experiment with these concepts to become proficient data analysts. Remember, practice is key! Applying the appropriate data structure to real-world data challenges greatly enhances analytical capabilities. Data relationships are also crucial in managing and understanding our data. The diverse forms of relationships between data sets enable us to better understand, manage, and manipulate them.

Likewise, data relationships are pivotal in managing and understanding our data. The diverse forms of relationships between data sets enable us to better understand, manage, and manipulate information to derive useful insights. They allow for a better grip on the nature of the information, aiding in maintaining the accuracy and consistency of data. The core types of relationships are “Many to One”, “One to One”, and “Many to Many” and we have read how each carries a distinct structure and function which serves to maintain data integrity and streamline data operations. Understanding the relationship type can guide us in handling duplicates, enhancing our ability to make better, data-driven decisions. By carefully observing and utilizing these relationships, we can significantly improve the quality of our data management efforts.

Data structures are crucial tools for analysts working with data, as they provide various ways to efficiently organise and manipulate data. Understanding these fundamental data structures enables analysts to tackle complex data analysis tasks and develop efficient algorithms. By applying appropriate data structures to real-world data challenges, analytical capabilities can be significantly enhanced.

Similarly, data relationships play a pivotal role in managing and understanding data. Establishing relationships between datasets can help to reduce data duplication, ensure consistency, and improve overall data management. By carefully observing and utilising these relationships, analysts can significantly improve the quality of their data management efforts and make better, data-driven decisions.

KEY TAKEAWAYS

In this chapter, we have delved into the world of data structures and data relationships, both of which are crucial in the field of data analysis. Data structures are fundamental concepts in computer science that facilitate effective data manipulation, while data relationships help us understand, manage, and manipulate information to derive useful insights. Let's explore these concepts in detail. Below are the key takeaways:

Data Structures:

- **Variables:** Variables are storage locations that hold values or data. They are the building blocks of data manipulation and can store different types of information, such as numbers, text, dates, or Boolean values. By assigning appropriate names to variables, analysts can easily identify and work with specific pieces of data, making it easier to reference and modify data throughout the analysis.
- **Data Tables:** Data tables, also known as datasets, are structured ways to store and organize data. They consist of rows and columns, where each row represents a record or observation, and each column represents a specific attribute or variable. Data tables provide a tabular format that allows for efficient data manipulation, filtering, sorting, and analysis. Popular tools for working with data tables include spreadsheet software like Microsoft Excel and Google Sheets.

- **Lists:** Lists are ordered collections of elements or items. Unlike data tables, lists are typically one-dimensional and can contain elements of different data types. They are flexible and allow for dynamic resizing, making them suitable for scenarios where the number of elements may change over time. Lists are often used to perform iterative operations or store data sequentially.
- **Arrays:** Arrays are similar to lists, as they also store collections of elements or variables. However, arrays have a fixed size and hold elements of the same data type. This fixed size provides efficient access and manipulation of elements within the array. Arrays are widely used in data analysis and programming languages to store large volumes of similar data and are especially useful for numerical computations and algorithms.
- **Key-Value Pairs:** Key-value pairs represent a data structure that associates a unique key with a corresponding value. Keys act as identifiers and provide a way to access and retrieve specific values from the data structure. Key-value pairs are often used in scenarios where fast data retrieval is required, such as dictionaries or lookup tables. They are particularly useful for linking data tables and ensuring data integrity.
- **Hash Tables:** Hash tables, also known as hash maps, are a type of data structure that provides efficient insertion, deletion, and retrieval of key-value pairs. They utilize a hashing function to map keys to an index or position within an underlying array, allowing for fast access to values based on their keys. Hash tables are widely used in various

applications, such as caching, indexing, and implementing associative arrays.

Data Relationships:

- **Many-to-One Relationships:** In a Many-to-One relationship, a key may appear multiple times in one table but only once in another. This implies that a single record from one table is associated with multiple records from another. Many-to-one relationships are crucial in identifying duplicate data and flagging potential inconsistencies and inaccuracies in data.
- **One-to-One Relationships:** A one-to-One relationship represents a scenario where each key appears only once in each table. Each entry in one table corresponds uniquely and exclusively to a single entry in another table. One-to-one relationships offer an easy means of managing duplicates because each entry should only appear once in each table.
- **Many-to-Many Relationships: Many-to-many** relationships signify that each key may appear multiple times in both tables. While Many-to-Many relationships offer flexibility in data organisation, they can often lead to data complexity and redundancy. They necessitate a "link" or "junction" table to prevent data redundancy and preserve overall data integrity.

Navigating and understanding the diverse landscape of database types is crucial for novice analysts. This is because each type offers unique advantages and disadvantages, making them suitable for specific use cases. Understanding the characteristics of the above-mentioned databases empowers us to make informed decisions when it comes to data storage and management in various contexts. By matching the right database type with the requirements of their projects, analysts can optimize performance, scalability, and data insights.

Data structures and relationships are essential for efficient data analysis. Understanding them enables analysts to tackle complex tasks and make data-driven decisions. By applying appropriate structures, analytical capabilities can be enhanced. Relationships can reduce duplication and improve data management.

chapter 7

UNDERSTANDING DATA TYPES AND FUNCTIONS TO BUILD DATA MODELS

I have battled a little with why some of the data behaved differently during my analysis. It became clear that this was common to novice analysts. As a novice analyst, understanding different data types was crucial to effectively analyse and interpret data. This knowledge burdened me, and I had to help others overcome this stage. Over the years I have helped many colleagues understand the different data types. In this chapter, let us explore the most common data types and highlight how best to handle each type and the functions best suited for each data type. Additionally, I hope to assist you with the advantages and disadvantages of each data type to help you gain a solid foundation in data analysis. Especially considering that analysts are not always in control of the data that they get.

COMMON DATA TYPES

There are common data types that I frequently analyse. This includes making analysis using (1) decimals data, (2) integers, (3) percentages, (4) date formatted data, (5) time formatted data, (6) date time (combining data and time), (7) text, (8) location, and (9) Boolean data – data that gives users two options such as yes/no, true/false, etcetera (They are stored the same way as Boolean, and we choose how we want this data presented). However, not all data is numerical or simply text-based. Before we start with analysis, I would recommend that we define data types for each column (variable) to optimise the amount of memory being used to store the data.

Various types could bring good insights into your analysis. It also depends on the choice of software being used or the needs of the top management (Manco/Exco). The software will also be able to understand how to manipulate the values. Some software does a good job of defining data for us, like Excel. But Excel doesn't get all the data types correct every time. This is because each data type behaves differently. I would like to discuss (1) Numeric data (decimals, integers, percentages, etc. that could be continuous or discrete), (2) categorical data (ordinal and nominal), (3) text data, and (4) time series data.

Numeric Data

Numeric data represent quantitative values and are further categorised into continuous and discrete subtypes. These are continuous or discrete numeric data. I have tried to explain this below for your convenience.

- **Continuous Numeric Data:** Continuous numeric data can take on any value within a range and allows for fractional values. It is data that shows where you are on the infinite range of numbers. Examples include temperature, height, and time. To handle continuous numeric data, statistical measures such as mean, median, and standard deviation can be employed. These statistical tools allow us to get a sense of the data. The advantages of using continuous numeric data include a high level of precision and detailed analysis. However, the disadvantage is that handling a large amount of continuous data can be computationally intensive.
- **Discrete Numeric Data:** Discrete numeric data consists of whole numbers or countable values. Examples include the number of products sold, the number of website visits, or the number of employees in a company. Although you could use statistical measures to understand the data, the common techniques to handle this data include frequency distributions, histograms, and bar charts. It makes it easier to see and understand these charts. Advantages include ease of interpretation and straightforward analysis. The disadvantage of using discrete data is that it may lack precision when compared to continuous data. This means you might not know whether selling ten apples is good or

bad but continuous data would tell you that forty degrees is a higher temperature.

Categorical Data

Categorical data is used to show/represent distinct categories or groups. This type of data is divided into two subtypes namely nominal and ordinal. I have also given a little description below to aid with understanding.

- **Nominal Categorical Data:** Nominal categorical data does not have any inherent order or ranking. You can rank it in the way that suits your analysis. Examples could be analysing data about gender, colours, or product categories. Neither gender is greater than the other, nor colours. You are free to order as you prefer. I would advise that we handle nominal categorical data by creating frequency tables, bar charts, or pie charts. The advantages of this data type are their ease of interpretation and visual representation. However, the disadvantage is that nominal data cannot be subjected to mathematical operations such as addition or subtraction.
- **Ordinal Categorical Data:** Ordinal categorical data has a predefined order or ranking. This means you must go through one before another, but it is not numerical all the time. Examples are comparing the educational levels of a group of individuals (e.g., primary, middle school, high school, university, professional), survey ratings (e.g., satisfaction levels), or product ratings. I'm assuming you have come across this type of data more often than not. I handle ordinal categorical data using techniques such as

rank order and cumulative frequency. The advantages of ordinal data include the ability to establish relative differences between the data you are analysing. However, the magnitude of differences between categories may not be accurately represented and thus could be a disadvantage.

Text Data

Text data includes unstructured textual information such as customer reviews, social media posts, or survey responses. This is data that is becoming popular in the analysis since Exco discovered that customers could be represented using more than numerical data. Analysing text data often involves techniques like Natural Language Processing (NLP), sentiment analysis, and text mining. The discovery of GPT4[57] has created waves in 2022 and 2023 for this reason. Businesses finally had access to a tool that could interpret customer needs better than data stored in SQL databases. It all depends on how text data will be used to empower both the marketing and sales teams/functions. The advantages of text data analysis include understanding customer sentiment, identifying trends, and extracting insights. The disadvantage of working with text data is that it can be challenging due to its complexity and ambiguity.

[57] GPT-4 vs. GPT-3.5: 5 Key Differences Explained - The Tech Edvocate - While much is still unknown about GPT-4 and the validity of GPT-3.5, it's clear that GPT models will continue to evolve and become more powerful. Businesses and industries that rely on natural language processing capabilities should carefully consider these key differences when making decisions about using AI technology. With new capabilities come new challenges and considerations, so it's important to stay informed about the latest developments in AI language models.

Time Series Data

Time series data represents observations collected over a sequence of equally spaced time intervals. These observations become statistically significant when collected over thirty observation points. We can thus use this to understand what happened historically and predict better what might happen next. Examples of time series data include stock market prices, weather data, or website traffic. Analysing time series data is exciting. I used techniques like trend analysis, seasonality detection, and forecasting. Seasonality detection and forecasting are available in the data analysis feature in Excel. I would encourage us to play around with this feature and increase our proficiency. The advantages of using time series data include the ability to identify patterns and make predictions. The disadvantage is that this data type can be influenced by various external factors, making it susceptible to outliers and anomalies.

NUMBER, TEXT, DATE, AND BOOLEAN FUNCTIONS

Do you still remember being asked to write a formula in Excel and then being baffled not knowing which one was appropriate? Well, I still do. I remember how I dreaded vlookups and a loop of infested if statements trying to get results. Well, in the world of data analysis, functions play a vital role in extracting valuable insights from raw data. Functions enable analysts like me to perform various calculations, manipulations, and transformations on data sets. I reflect here on how far I have come in my analyst journey.

I will also explore four essential types of functions analysts frequently utilise. This includes:

- Number Functions,
- Text Functions,
- Date Functions, and
- Boolean Functions.

I learnt how to use most of these functions in Excel and I then made tweaks to achieve similar results when using other software applications. Understanding these functions will equip more analysts with the necessary tools to work with different types of data and derive meaningful conclusions.

Number Functions

Number Functions are essential for performing mathematical operations on numerical data. These functions are common mainly when manually calculating descriptive statistics. They enable analysts to conduct calculations, aggregations, and comparisons. Some commonly used Number Functions include: (1) SUM: Which adds up a range of numbers, (2) AVERAGE: Which calculates the average of a set of numbers, (3) MAX: Which returns the maximum value from a range of numbers, (4) MIN: Returns the minimum value from a range of numbers, (5) COUNT: Counts the number of cells in a range that contain numbers. Number Functions are particularly useful when analysing financial data, sales figures, or any other numeric data that requires computation or statistical analysis.

Text Functions

Text Functions were useful when I wanted to manipulate and analyse textual data. I often encountered situations where I needed to extract specific information from text, combine different text values, or perform comparisons based on text conditions. I can recommend we start by using the following Text Functions: (1) CONCATENATE: Joins multiple text strings together, (2) LEN: Determines the length of a text string, (3) LEFT/RIGHT: Extracts a specific number of characters from the left or right side of a text string, (4) FIND: Finds the position of a specific character or text within a text string, (5) SUBSTITUTE: Replaces specific text within a text string with new text.

Text Functions become handy and invaluable when working with data such as customer/employee names, branch details, product descriptions, or any other textual information. Using the above functions will allow us to focus on what matters the most. There are many instances where I had to use more than one Text Function in one formula.

Date Functions

Date Functions are designed to handle dates and perform various operations on them. This type works well when your data field/column has been formatted as a Date. I used these functions when I needed to extract specific components from dates, calculate time differences, or group data based on dates. Some Date Functions I am fond of include (1) TODAY: Returns the current date, (2) DateAdd() Today() DateDiff() Month() IsDate() YEAR/MONTH/DAY: Extracts the year, month, or day from a given date, (3) DATEDIF: Calculates the difference between two dates, (4) EOMONTH: Returns the last day of the month for a given date, (5) WEEKDAY: Determines the day of the week for a given date. You can also feel free to explore DATEADD, DATEDIFF, or ISDATE to be ready for date-related analysis especially when analysing time series data, tracking trends, or performing any investigation that involves temporal information.

Boolean Functions

Boolean Functions are used to evaluate logical conditions and return either true or false values. I often use Boolean Functions to make comparisons, test conditions, or filter data based on specific criteria. They are what we normally get from management questions when analysis is required. I normally replaced some words in the questions with Boolean functions. My favourite Boolean Functions are (1) IF: Which performs a logical test and returns different values based on the result, (2) AND/OR: Which evaluates multiple conditions and returns true or false based on the logical outcome, (3) NOT: Inverts the logical value of a given condition, (4) COUNTIF: Counts the number of cells in a range that meet specific criteria, and (5) ISBLANK: which is ideal to check if a cell is empty or contains a value.

Boolean Functions are important when we want to compute values for decision-making, data filtering, and creating logical statements in data analysis. Boolean values describe whether a certain condition is true or false. There are four comparison operators I have used to compute Boolean values. These operators are: (1) equals "=", (2) greater than ">", (3) less than "<", and (4) not equal to "≠" or "!=" in SQL queries. Boolean values, whether "True" or

"False", are variables that could be used in Boolean Functions. An example could be IF (LOGICAL_TEST, OUTCOME_IF_TRUE, OUTCOME_IF_FALSE). The application of Logical Functions is often referred to as Boolean Logic.

DATA TYPES & FUNCTIONS

As an analyst, I rely heavily on functions when analysing data. Functions are essential in extracting valuable insights from raw data and are found in analytical software applications such as Excel. They allow me to perform various calculations, manipulations, and transformations on data sets, making them powerful tools for extracting insights from different types of data. To perform complex calculations, transformations, and evaluations, I need to understand four types of functions: Number Functions, Text Functions, Date Functions, and Boolean Functions. By utilising these functions effectively, I can uncover valuable information, identify patterns, and make data-driven decisions.

Novice analysis might benefit from understanding the different types of data. The common data types are (1) decimals data, (2) integers, (3) percentages, (4) date formatted data, (5) time formatted data, (6) date time (combining data and time), (7) text, (8) location, and (9) Boolean data. I have thoroughly enjoyed sharing my understanding of (1) Numeric data (decimals, integers, percentages, etc. that could be continuous or discrete), (2) categorical data (ordinal and nominal), (3) text data, and (4) time series data.

I still believe that understanding different data types is essential for effective data analysis. By recognising the characteristics, advantages, and disadvantages of each data type, a novice analyst could choose appropriate techniques and tools to handle and interpret data accurately. Remember that combining multiple data types and employing advanced analytical methods can provide richer insights and support more informed decision-making especially when this is done using data models.

CREATING EFFECTIVE DATA MODELS

In the age of information, data has become a priceless asset that organisations utilise to make strategic decisions, predict trends, and understand customer behaviour. We have all witnessed how over the years data has become the lifeblood of organisations worldwide, and one of the most important components of any data analysis or business intelligence operation is the creation of a data model. Central to harnessing the full potential of this data is the concept of 'data models'. In simplest terms, a data model is a framework that determines how data is stored, organised, and manipulated. It consists of two or more tables that are interconnected via relationships. Data models provide a method to organize and understand complex sets of data, acting as the blueprint for how data is connected and used. At its most basic, a data model consists of two or more tables that are interconnected through relationships.

UNDERSTANDING DATA MODELS

A data model is a conceptual representation of data structures required for a database and used in database design. It defines how data is interconnected, processed, and stored in the system. The model describes the organisation of the data to certain rules and definitions. At its core, a data model provides a systematic and logical view of data that enhances its comprehensibility and usability. The primary components of a data model are entities (tables), attributes (fields), and relationships. Entities represent real-world objects or events, while attributes provide detailed descriptions of these entities.

The relationships link these entities, demonstrating how they interact with each other. In the realm of data warehousing, there are two key types of tables: (1) fact tables and (2) dimension tables. Fact tables primarily contain measurements about events or transactions. They are the core of a star schema in a data warehouse, surrounded by dimension tables. On the other hand, Dimension tables contain attributes that help describe these events or transactions in more detail. Before we delve into fact and dimensional tables, let us explore why we should consider using data models.

Benefits of Using Data Models

- *Improved Data Quality:* Data models enhance the quality of data by providing a structured and consistent format for data entry. They also ensure that data is consistent and accurate which is important for having a single truth. This leads to reduced errors and inconsistencies in data. How? By defining the relationships between data, a model can enforce data integrity rules and prevent inaccurate data from being entered into the system.

- *Efficient Data Retrieval:* The logical structure of a data model enhances data retrieval and manipulation. With a well-designed model, we can swiftly navigate through vast amounts of data and retrieve necessary information. Furthermore, they can optimise how queries are executed by providing a structure that can be more efficiently navigated and searched. By defining relationships between data elements, models can prevent unnecessary data duplication, saving storage space and improving system performance.
- *Simplified Data Integration:* A robust data model allows for easy integration of data from various sources, making it an indispensable tool for large-scale data analysis.
- *Improved Business Decisions:* By making complex data more understandable, data models can help organisations make more informed decisions. They provide a clearer understanding of the relationships and patterns in the data, which can lead to valuable business insights.
- *Enhanced Communication:* Data models provide a visual representation of data structures, which can improve communication among different teams within an organisation. This is because they act as a shared language for business and IT teams. They can help bridge the gap between technical implementation and business requirements, improving collaboration and communication across the organisation. All of this depends heavily on what

has been documented in the Business Requirement Document (BRD).

Challenges in Using Data Models

- *Complexity:* Designing an effective data model can be a complex task, especially for large datasets with many entities and relationships. They require a deep understanding of the data, its structure, and how it is used within the organisation. Inaccurate or incomplete models can lead to errors and inconsistencies. I remember how I battled managing finance data models. No amount of documentation could assist especially when things weren't going right.
- *Time-Consuming:* The process of creating a comprehensive data model can be time-consuming, requiring a significant amount of planning and conceptualisation. It would be advisable to take time to properly do this.
- *Rigidity:* Once a data model is in place, it can be difficult to change. This rigidity can be a problem as business needs and data sources evolve. We experience this when we have new data to import and our model almost collapses. Highly technical analysts could create processes for additional data tables to the model.
- *Maintenance:* As business needs evolve, data models may need to be updated or revised. You can imagine the benefit of having team members to assist in maintaining the model. This can involve significant effort and technical

expertise. It is not recommended that you do this by yourself.

UNDERSTANDING FACT TABLES AND DIMENSION TABLES

Now that you have seen both sides of the data model, I think we could resume our conversation. When we talk about a data model, we often refer to two fundamental types of tables: Fact tables and Dimension tables. "What are these?", you may be asking.

A **Fact Table** is the centre of the data model, containing quantifiable data about the events or transactions your business deals with. Fact tables often include numerical data, such as sales figures, that can be analysed and aggregated to provide valuable insights. They are typically designed with many foreign keys corresponding to the primary keys of the surrounding dimension tables.

Dimension Tables, on the other hand, are used to describe the 'dimensions' or contexts of the facts. For example, if your fact table records sales data, your dimension tables might include information about the products being sold, the time of sale, the location of the sale, and the customer who made the purchase. These tables provide the who, what, where, when, and why to complement the numerical data in the fact table.

Data has and will continue to become a priceless asset that organisations utilize to make strategic decisions, predict trends, and understand customer behaviour. Data modelling is a critical process that helps organise and make sense of complex datasets. While the process can be time-consuming and sometimes complex, the rewards are great. Although data models come with their challenges, their benefits in improving data quality, performance, decision-making, and communication are invaluable. It improves data quality, enables efficient data retrieval, and simplifies data integration. By understanding the different components of a data model, especially fact and dimension tables, analysts can effectively harness the power of data to drive meaningful insights and business decisions. As a novice analyst, understanding how to build and use data models effectively will be vital in your data analysis toolkit.

KEY TAKEAWAYS

In Chapter 7, we have discussed the importance of understanding different data types and functions in data analysis. I also shared my experiences as a novice analyst and how I learned to handle various data types effectively. The chapter covers the following key points:

- **Common Data Types:** The chapter identifies several common data types that are frequently analysed, including decimals data, integers, percentages, date formatted data, time formatted data, date-time (combining data and time), text, location, and Boolean data. Not all data is numerical or text-based, and it's essential to define data types for each variable to optimise memory usage.
- **Numeric Data:** Numeric data represents quantitative values and can be continuous or discrete. Continuous numeric data allows for any value within a range and can have fractional values, while discrete numeric data consists of whole numbers or countable values. Statistical measures like mean, median, and standard deviation are used for continuous data, while frequency distributions and histograms are common for discrete data.
- **Categorical Data:** Categorical data represents distinct categories or groups and is divided into nominal and ordinal subtypes. Nominal data has no inherent order, while ordinal data has a predefined order. Nominal data can be analysed using frequency tables and charts, while

ordinal data can be analysed using rank order and cumulative frequency techniques.

- **Text Data:** Text data includes unstructured textual information and is becoming popular in analysis. Techniques like Natural Language Processing (NLP) and sentiment analysis are used to analyse text data. It offers valuable insights into customer sentiment, trends, and opinions, but it can be challenging due to its complexity.
- **Time Series Data:** Time series data represents observations collected over equally spaced time intervals. Techniques like trend analysis, seasonality detection, and forecasting are used to analyse time series data. It allows for identifying patterns and making predictions but can be influenced by external factors.
- **Number, Text, Date, and Boolean Functions:** Functions play a vital role in extracting insights from raw data. The author explores four essential types of functions used in data analysis: Number Functions, Text Functions, Date Functions, and Boolean Functions. These functions enable analysts to perform calculations, manipulations, and transformations on data sets.

What is crucial to remember from the chapter is that:

- Understanding different data types is crucial for effective data analysis. Novice analysts should familiarise themselves with the common data types and how to handle each type.
- Numeric data can be continuous (fractional values within a range) or discrete (whole numbers or countable values).

Different statistical measures and techniques are used for each type.

- Categorical data can be nominal (no inherent order) or ordinal (predefined order). The analysis methods differ for each subtype.
- Text data analysis involves techniques like NLP and sentiment analysis, offering valuable insights into customer sentiment and trends.
- Time series data allows for understanding historical patterns and making predictions, but it can be affected by external factors.
- Number, Text, Date, and Boolean Functions are essential tools for extracting insights from raw data. Each function type serves specific purposes in data analysis.
- Data models provide a framework for storing, organising, and manipulating data. They consist of entities (tables), attributes (fields), and relationships. Fact tables contain quantifiable data about events, while dimension tables describe the context of facts.
- Data models offer various benefits, including improved data quality, efficient data retrieval, simplified data integration, and enhanced decision-making.
- Challenges in using data models include complexity, time consumption, rigidity, and maintenance requirements.
- Understanding data types, functions, and data models is crucial for effective data analysis and can lead to valuable business insights and informed decision-making.

Overall, mastering data types, functions, and data models is essential for any data analyst seeking to derive meaningful conclusions from data and provide valuable insights to their organisation.

chapter 8

GOOD VISUALS VS. BAD REPORTS IN DATA ANALYTICS

I have witnessed how bad reports create confusion in the boardroom, especially when the reports are badly made, or the team quickly comes to conclusions without properly engaging the audience. Thus, in the realm of analytics, effective communication of insights and information is crucial. It is in this case that visuals and dashboards play pivotal roles in presenting data concisely and meaningfully. However, for those new to the field, understanding the differences between visuals and dashboards, and their respective roles in conveying a data story, can be challenging.

The top management (Exco/Manco) might deem the team incompetent unnecessarily. All of this could have been avoided if the data team understood the right way to share insights with Exco/Manco. In this chapter, we will explore the concepts of visuals and dashboards, the significance of data storytelling, different chart types, the characteristics of good and bad visuals, essential design principles for Power BI, and a brief comparison between Power BI and Tableau.

WHAT IS A DATA STORY?

Before delving into visuals and dashboards, it's important to grasp the concept of a data story. Data storytelling is very similar to human storytelling but provides the added benefits of deeper insights and supporting evidence through graphs and charts. Through data storytelling, complicated information is simplified so that your audience can engage with your content and make critical decisions quickly and more confidently. A data story is a narrative that unfolds using data to provide insights, make informed decisions, or communicate a particular message. It involves structuring data in a logical sequence to engage the audience and encourage a deeper understanding of the information at hand.

According to the Power BI community[58], some benefits of successful data storytelling include:

---

[58] What is Data Storytelling and Data Storytelling Examples | Microsoft Power BI - Data storytelling is the concept of building a compelling narrative based on complex data and analytics that help tell your story and influence and inform a particular audience. Data storytelling is very similar to human storytelling but provides the added benefits of deeper insights and supporting evidence through graphs and charts. Through data storytelling, complicated information is simplified so that your audience can engage with your content and make critical decisions quicker and more confidently.

- Adding value to your data and insights,
- Interpreting complex information and highlighting essential key points for the audience,
- Providing a human touch to your data,
- Offering value to your audience and industry, and
- Building credibility as an industry and topic thought leader.

Data storytelling is the art of presenting data with a contextual narrative. There are a few different ways to present your data story. You might be asking "What are the best ways to present to top management?" at this point. We first need to understand the importance of data visuals in order to answer this question.

DATA VISUALS

Visuals refer to individual data visualisation using charts, graphs, maps, or infographics. They are used to present specific data points, trends, or comparisons. Visuals are often created using software tools like Power BI or Tableau and serve as building blocks for larger dashboards. I was first introduced to the power behind a good visual when I was doing sales operation reporting. There was a need for me and my direct reports to share daily sales stats with the national team. Many regional, area, and branch sales managers battled to interpret Excel files that we were initially sent by the sales analytics team. Through effective communication, I soon realised that none of the sales team loves to spend more time than they should on reading a report.

Constructing a data story that moves a person to take action can be a very powerful tool. Effective data storytelling can have a positive impact on people and your organisation.

There are many types of visuals. Using the right visual would convey a better message as compared to using an incompatible one. All of this depends on the proficiency level of the data team and the analytical ability of the audience. It becomes useless to present a complicated visual to an audience that requested a variance analysis. Let's first understand what the common chart types in data analysis are.

CHART TYPES

Charts are a common form of visual representation in data analytics. Different chart types cater to specific data characteristics and help convey information effectively. I would advise the data team to spend the greater part of the initial meeting gathering information about which reports your audience loves. Getting your hands on these types of reports would allow you the opportunity to know the best chart types to use. It might come as a surprise to novice analysts that not all chart types will give you good remarks.

There are various types also. Some widely used chart types include bar charts, line charts, pie charts, scatter plots, and heat maps. Each chart type has its strengths and is chosen based on the nature of the data and the message intended to be conveyed. Your audience might sometimes request a combination chart. The data team must be ready for whatever, otherwise your hard work might not be seen and thus deemed a bad report.

GOOD VS. BAD VISUALS

Creating effective visuals involves adhering to certain principles. Good visuals are clear, concise, and visually appealing. They emphasize the main message, avoid clutter, and provide context. I would thus strongly suggest that the data team send the reports in small parts to gauge which parts your audience/top management might be happy with. On the other hand, bad visuals lack clarity, confuse the audience, or fail to highlight the key insights. Common mistakes include using inappropriate chart types, overwhelming the visual with unnecessary details, or displaying misleading information.

The number one rule is that unless your audience requested a table, you don't bring Excel to the boardroom for presentation. You can export what you see in Excel to PDF so that it looks like a well-thought-out report. With that said some Exco/Manco members might deliberately ask you for a data dump. It might be due to experience, and they want to be in control again. Try to create another worksheet with visuals to showcase what you are capable of as a data team. You as the data team need to know what should not be done when you use BI tools like Power BI.

POWER BI/TABLEAU DESIGN PRINCIPLES

Power BI and Tableau have become popular data visualisation and BI tools. Most data analysts and visualisation specialists managed to handle the irritation of a drastic monthly update. We are now accustomed to the ribbon and some features found on the tool. Thus, following a set of design principles to enhance visual clarity and user experience would win the hearts of your audience. These principles include proper data modelling, establishing clear relationships between visual elements, maintaining consistent design styles, utilising appropriate colour schemes, and optimising the layout for better usability.

Having this flow of data and creating a good data story would guarantee most of your visuals are included in operational dashboards. I know some analysts prefer Power BI while others state that Tableau is well-designed and has better features. Your audience has got a better hand in choosing the tool than the data team – the customer is always right. Let us understand how the two tools, Power BI and Tableau, are ranked in the market.

Power BI vs. Tableau Rankings

Power BI and Tableau are both powerful data visualisation tools, each with strengths and weaknesses. While Power BI is known for its tight integration with the Microsoft ecosystem, ease of use, and cost-effectiveness, Tableau excels in data exploration, advanced analytics, and dashboard customisation. Rankings may vary depending on specific requirements and preferences, so it's essential to evaluate the needs of your audience when choosing between the two. You will see that I have dedicated an entire Chapter (9) to assist you in selecting the best tool for your team/project.

CHART TYPES: ENHANCING DATA VISUALIZATION FOR MAXIMUM CLARITY

In the world of data visualisation, choosing the right chart type plays a vital role in effectively conveying information to an audience. I have battled with this for a long time. You can imagine the meetings I conducted where I confused top management (Manco/Exco) because of mixed messages conveyed by my visuals/charts. While numerous chart types are available, it is crucial to select the most suitable one that communicates a message with absolute clarity. This is for us to delve into various chart types and their unique characteristics, allowing data visualisation specialists to make informed decisions about their visual representations.

Let us not confuse our audience and rather share information about how to be better at making effective visuals. In so doing, it would be better for us to provide (Part 1) an overview of each chart type followed by (Part 2) how we can focus the attention of our audience. We know the hidden messages in data, and we have the power to bring these messages to life or squander the opportunity.

Part 1: An Overview of Chart Types

- **Bar Chart**: The bar chart is a widely used chart type that presents data in rectangular bars, where the length of each bar corresponds to the value it represents. It is excellent for comparing discrete categories and their respective values. I used this to show trends especially to highlight seasonal peaks and floors (High and Lows). It is mostly well received by many meeting attendees. The downside is that not everyone is comfortable reading vertically. This could be solved by horizontal/vertical columns.

- **Column Chart**: Like the bar chart, the column chart represents data using vertical columns instead of horizontal bars. It shares the same characteristics and applications as the bar chart but provides a different visual perspective. We don't go wrong with this chart type because of most Exco/Manco members' preferences. We can highlight anomalies and also predict the shape of the next columns. Sometimes having a line instead of columns could do the trick.
- **Line or Area Chart**: The line chart displays data points connected by lines, while the area chart fills the area below the lines, providing a visual representation of cumulative data trends over time. They are particularly useful for illustrating trends, patterns, and changes in data. The other nice part about this is that they remove clutter and the line (or area under the line) is ideal to visualise moving averages. Sometimes we might want to show the composition of our numbers, especially the positives and negatives.
- **Waterfall Chart**: A waterfall chart demonstrates the cumulative effect of positive and negative values, displaying how an initial value increases or decreases over a series of intermediate values. This chart type is commonly used for financial data analysis and showcasing the contribution of different factors to a total. We also used waterfall charts to break down the numbers into categories.

But at times we might be asked to show a minimalist approach.

- **Card**: The card is a concise and minimalist chart type that showcases a single data point or a small set of data points, often used to display key metrics or summary information. We can also use this to highlight key metrics (KPIs) important to each Manco member. Imaging showing the headcount (HC) growth number on a card for the HR department. The number could be green when heading in the direction of strategy (increase or decrease HC) and red in the adverse direction. Sometimes we could be asked to show single data points in a group.
- **Scatter Chart**: Scatter charts represent data as a collection of individual data points plotted on a Cartesian coordinate system. They are effective for identifying relationships, clusters, or correlations between two variables. Following our HR department example, we could show HC growth by seniority on a plot. This will allow us to see movements.
- **Tornado Chart**: The tornado chart, also known as a butterfly chart or population pyramid, visualises the comparison of two variables using bars that extend in opposite directions. It is commonly used for comparing the positive and negative impacts of different factors.
- **Box & Whisker**: The box and whisker plot displays a statistical summary of a dataset, including median, quartiles, and outliers. You can see all of this on Datapoint. It is ideal for an audience that needs descriptive statistics per data point. This is because it provides a concise representation of the distribution and variability of the data.

I have only learned about this in technical analysis. Perhaps investment analysis might be using the Box & Whisker chart a lot.

- **Tree Diagram**: Tree diagrams represent hierarchical structures or relationships between categories. They are commonly used to visualise organisational structures, decision trees, or hierarchical data. My Exco loved this type of diagram to show vendor spend analysis. We could easily see who the biggest vendor is in my category and how much has been spent on them. Depending on your preferences, the diagram groups small values together as other categories.
- **Heatmap**: Heatmaps use colour variations to represent values in a matrix format. It might look like a tree diagram at first and you will soon recognise that each block size is not a representation of the amount. They are excellent for displaying large datasets, identifying patterns, and visualising the intensity of values across different categories. Try this chart if you want to show areas that have a high number of backdated journals compared to others without using heat–colour grading.
- **Map**: Maps present data geographically, allowing for spatial analysis and insights. I was excited to see this feature on Power BI after struggling with Power View for a long time. They are used to display regional or global data, such as population density, sales distribution, or geographic patterns. I used this to remind Exco/Manco about the location of a market being analysed. Having a visual to show the location often changes perspective.

- **Doughnuts or Pie Charts**: Doughnuts and pie charts represent data as sectors of a circle, with each sector proportional to the value it represents. They are useful for illustrating the composition or distribution of data categories. They are also preferable if you want to highlight something. But before we could start using this chart type, let us spend some time discussing how visuals grab attention.

Part 2: Focusing Audience Attention Using visuals

To captivate and engage the audience effectively, data visualisation specialists can employ the following two techniques (highlighting values and presenting & comparing values)

A. HIGHLIGHTING VALUES

- Colour can be a good attention grabber, using vibrant or contrasting colours to draw attention to specific data points or categories;
- Enclosure of important data points or categories within shapes, such as boxes or circles, to emphasize them;
- Shaping can also be useful when utilising distinct shapes or symbols to highlight significant data points or categories; and
- Position on what we want to talk about/ critical data points or categories in prominent positions within the visual to attract attention.

B. PRESENTING & COMPARING VALUES

- Use the length of bars or lines to showcase the magnitude or scale of values which could be ideal for bar and column charts;
- Vary the size of visual elements, such as circles or icons, to represent different values or proportions;
- Annotation could be useful by adding text or labels to provide additional context or explanation for data points or categories;
- Ordering your data can make a huge difference thus try and arrange data points or categories in a specific order to convey a particular narrative or emphasize comparisons;
- Display average values or reference lines to enable better understanding and comparison;
- Use dual axes to visualise two different scales or units on the same chart, allowing for direct comparison.

HOW ARE VISUALS COMMUNICATING?

Choosing the right chart type plays a vital role in effectively conveying information to an audience. Now we don't have to battle with data visualisation anymore, especially after understanding chart types. Choosing the right chart type and employing effective visualisation techniques are crucial elements in conveying data with absolute clarity. By understanding the characteristics and applications of various chart types and implementing visual techniques to focus audience attention, data visualisation specialists can ensure that their visualisations effectively communicate insights and drive meaningful understanding.

Remember, the best chart is often the simplest one that conveys the intended message.

I would suggest that the data team understand visuals that speak to the audience. There have been a lot of good reports failing to connect with the audience due to the choice of visuals. Great visuals were put together to create a good report. Key insights about the report are then extracted (pinned) to create a good dashboard. Visuals and dashboards are vital components in the data analytics realm. Visuals, such as charts and graphs, provide focused insights into specific data points, while dashboards serve as comprehensive collections of visuals to tell a broader data story. Creating effective visuals involves selecting appropriate chart types and adhering to design principles that enhance clarity and user experience. Power BI and Tableau are two leading data visualisation tools, each with its unique features and strengths. Understanding these concepts will enable newcomers to effectively communicate data-driven insights and engage their audience through compelling visual storytelling.

KEY TAKEAWAYS

Chapter 8 discussed the importance of effective communication in the realm of analytics, particularly in the context of data visualisation. This chapter emphasised the significance of data storytelling and how visuals and dashboards play pivotal roles in presenting data concisely and meaningfully.

What is crucial to remember from the chapter is that:

1. **Data Storytelling:** Data storytelling is the art of presenting data in a narrative form, using visuals and supporting evidence to provide insights, make informed decisions, or communicate a specific message. Successful data storytelling adds value to data and insights, interprets complex information for the audience, and builds credibility as an industry thought leader.

2. **Data Visuals:** Visuals refer to individual data visualizations like charts, graphs, maps, or infographics. They present specific data points, trends, or comparisons and are essential building blocks for creating larger dashboards.

3. **Chart Types:** Different chart types cater to specific data characteristics and help convey information effectively. Common chart types include bar charts, line charts, pie charts, scatter plots, and heat maps. Choosing the right chart type is crucial for effective communication.

4. **Good vs. Bad Visuals:** Good visuals are clear, concise, visually appealing, and emphasise the main message without overwhelming the audience. In contrast, bad visuals lack clarity, confuse the audience, or display misleading information. Adhering to design principles is essential for creating effective visuals.

5. **Power BI and Tableau Design Principles:** Following design principles enhances visual clarity and user experience in Power BI and Tableau. Principles include proper data modelling, establishing clear relationships between visual elements, maintaining consistent design styles, utilising appropriate colour schemes, and optimising layout for better usability. Power BI and Tableau are powerful data visualisation tools, each with its strengths and weaknesses. Choosing the right tool depends on specific requirements and audience preferences.

6. **Focusing Audience Attention Using Visuals:** To captivate and engage the audience effectively, visualisation specialists can use techniques like highlighting values, presenting and comparing values, and employing various visual elements.

7. **Choosing the Right Chart Type:** The choice of the right chart type plays a vital role in effectively conveying information to the audience. Data visualisation specialists need to understand the characteristics and applications of various chart types to communicate insights.

8. **Visuals and Dashboards:** Visuals provide focused insights into specific data points, while dashboards serve as comprehensive collections of visuals to tell a broader data story. Understanding the right visuals to use for specific audiences is crucial for effective communication.

In conclusion, effective data storytelling and data visualisation are crucial for communicating data-driven insights and engaging the audience. Understanding chart types, design principles, and the differences between visuals and dashboards can help data teams avoid confusion and present data in a meaningful way to management committees and stakeholders.

chapter 9

A COMPARATIVE OVERVIEW OF COMMON DATA VISUALISATION TOOLS

Data visualisation plays a vital role in transforming complex data into easily understandable and actionable insights. In Chapter 8, I highlighted the importance of telling a story to management. With a plethora of data visualisation tools available in the market, organisations have numerous options to choose from based on their requirements. Knowing how each tool compares with others would assist management with buying decisions. In this article, we will explore and compare twelve popular data visualisation tools, namely Tableau, Power BI, Microsoft Excel, MicroStrategy, Qlik, Looker, Sisense, Dunbas BI, Adaptive Insights, Analytics, Plotly, and Python. We will explore their histories, advantages, disadvantages, and market shares.

MICROSOFT EXCEL

Microsoft Excel[59] has been a staple spreadsheet tool since its inception in 1987. It has evolved to include data visualisation capabilities. This was with the integration of Power Pivot, Power View, and Power Query. Today, Copilot in Excel helps us analyse and explore our data so we can make the best decisions. Copilot[60] helps us identify trends, propose what-if scenarios, suggest ideas for improving your business, and will even build everything into an easy-to-read dashboard.

The advantage of this tool is widely available and familiar to many users. It offers basic charting and visualisation options, suitable for simple data analysis tasks. The disadvantages of Excel are its limitations in handling large datasets and its lack of advanced visualisation functionalities compared to dedicated tools. Despite the above, Excel remains a popular choice for basic data visualisation, especially among non-technical users.

---

[59] Microsoft Excel - Wikipedia - Microsoft Excel is a spreadsheet editor developed by Microsoft for Windows, macOS, Android, iOS and iPadOS. It features calculation or computation capabilities, graphing tools, pivot tables, and a macro programming language called Visual Basic for Applications (VBA). Excel forms part of the Microsoft 365 suite of software.

[60] Microsoft 365 Copilot – Microsoft Adoption - Microsoft 365 Copilot combines the power of large language models (LLMs) with your organisation's data – all in the flow of work – to turn your words into one of the most powerful productivity tools on the planet. It works alongside popular Microsoft 365 Apps such as Word, Excel, PowerPoint, Outlook, Teams, and more. Copilot provides real-time intelligent assistance, enabling users to enhance their creativity, productivity, and skills.

TABLEAU

Tableau[61] was founded in 2003 and quickly gained popularity for its intuitive drag-and-drop interface and powerful analytics capabilities. Their visual analytics platform promises to transform the way people use data to solve problems. The latest tool tools bring analytics to life with Artificial Intelligence (AI) and personalised insights – Say hello to Tableau GPT and Tableau Pulse, the next generation of Tableau. Tableau has established itself as a leader in the data visualisation market, with a substantial market share.

The advantages of Tableau are that it offers a wide range of visualisations, interactive dashboards, and seamless data integration. It provides robust features for data exploration and storytelling. However, the disadvantages include being expensive for small businesses, and some advanced functionalities require technical expertise.

POWER BI

Power BI[62] is a business analytics tool developed by Microsoft and launched in 2013. It is known for its tight integration with other Microsoft products. The tool helps us do more with less using an end-to-end BI platform to create a single source of truth, uncover

[61] About Tableau: Helping people see and understand data - Tableau helps people see and understand data with visual analytics platform is transforming the way people use data to solve problems. This is why organisations of all sizes trust Tableau to help them be more data-driven.

[62] What is Power BI? Definition and Overview | Microsoft Power BI - Power BI is a unified, scalable platform for self-service and enterprise business intelligence (BI). Connect to and visualize any data, and seamlessly infuse the visuals into the apps you use every day.

more powerful insights, and translate them into impact. Recently, Microsoft has incorporated their AI product, Copilot, into Power BI. This helps us uncover the full potential of our data using next-generation AI tools. We can describe the insights we need or ask a question about our data and Copilot analyses and pulls the right data into a report—easily turning data into actionable insights.

The advantages include excellent integration capabilities, a user-friendly interface, and a broad range of data connectors. It also provides strong collaboration features. The disadvantages are that advanced features may require a learning curve, and the free version has limited functionality. Besides this drawback, Power BI has gained significant market share, benefiting from its association with the Microsoft ecosystem. Ecosystem integration contributed to its popularity despite being launched a decade after Tableau.

MICROSTRATEGY:

MicroStrategy[63] was founded in 1989 and has grown into a comprehensive business intelligence platform, including data visualisation. MicroStrategy ONE is their latest and most complete and expansive analytics platform yet. Not only is it fully modern, open, and cloud-powered—it's the single platform for all analytics use cases. The tool promises to unleash the power of data to create a competitive advantage and trust in insights at scale. They

---

[63] Business Intelligence & Analytics Solutions (microstrategy.com) - MicroStrategy ONE is the platform for all future innovation moving forward. And the global engineering teams are pivoting to what's next. MicroStrategy is dedicated to the design of cutting-edge features that enhance intelligence and influence through analytics. Go behind the scenes with smart workflows, augmented experiences, and the debut of Generative AI. It's time to go all in.

claim to be the only platform in the world that can do it all with maximum performance.

Their mantra is "Based On Fact, Not Instinct" thus they don't believe in guessing games. They believe in (1) data that replaces guessing with knowing; (2) challenging the status quo with data to back it up; (3) organisations using data to fuel innovation and come up with the next big thing. No noise, no distractions. Focus and make every decision count. MicroStrategy has a notable presence in the enterprise market but faces stiff competition from other tools.

The advantage of using MicroStrategy is the ability to provide robust enterprise-grade analytics capabilities, scalability, and security features. However good it may seem; the tool can also be complex to set up and requires technical expertise. The learning curve may be steep for non-technical users.

QLIK

Qlik[64], developed by Qlik, was introduced in 1993. It gained recognition for its associative data indexing technology. Qlik Cloud, their latest offering, promises organisations the ability to seize every business moment with their AI-driven data integration and analytics cloud platform. They have introduced a suite of new

[64] Qlik | Analytics & Data Integration Platform - Qlik helps enterprises around the world move faster, work smarter, and lead the way forward with an end-to-end solution for getting value out of data. Our Active Intelligence Platform® is the only one on the market that allows for open-ended, curiosity-driven exploration, giving everyone – at any skill level – the ability to make real discoveries that lead to real outcomes and transformative changes.

OpenAI[65] connectors to expand organisational analytics possibilities, get new natural language insights, and add third-party data to the models in real time.

The advantage is that Qlik offers powerful data exploration capabilities, associative search, and data storytelling features. It provides a seamless user experience. On the contrary, some users find Qlik's interface less intuitive compared to other tools, and the pricing can be a deterrent for small businesses. Despite this, Qlik still holds a significant market share, particularly in the business intelligence and data analytics space.

LOOKER

Looker was founded in 2011 and acquired by Google in 2020. It is known for its cloud-based data platform and embedded analytics capabilities. Looker Studio is built on top of Google Drive, so you can share your reports and data sources the same way you share docs, spreadsheets, and slides. We can collaborate by sharing with edit permission or just share your insights in "view only" mode. Either way, other people never have direct access to your data. Because of this, Looker has been gaining traction, especially in the cloud-based analytics market.

The advantage of choosing Looker is its focus on collaboration, sharing, and embedding data visualizations. It offers a powerful API[66] for customization and integration. The disadvantage is that

---

[65] OpenAI - OpenAI is an AI research and deployment company with a mission to ensure that artificial general intelligence benefits all of humanity.

[66] API stands for application programming interface. It is a set of rules that allow various applications to communicate with each other. APIs act as a mediator that facilitates data transfers between

the tool may have a steeper learning curve compared to other tools, and some users may find the interface less intuitive. I believe organisations in the Google ecosystem might prefer Looker the way Power Bi is being appreciated.

SISENSE

Sisense[67] was established in 2004 and is known for its easy-to-use and scalable business intelligence platform. It was founded in Tel Aviv with the idea that data analytics can be made fluent, easy, and fast through technical innovation. The tool is scalable, secure, and seamless. Furthermore, it promised to (1) Infuse AI-driven analytics into your products and business applications; (2) Live/direct connection with Excel or Google Sheets directly to your data model and collaborate on Teams or Slack; (3) Leverage code-free to code-first tools for deeper analysis across all skill levels; (4) Seamlessly integrate into your existing tech stack and connect to all data; (4) Augment every analysis with AI and machine learning for forward-looking intelligence without the need for tech expertise; and (5) Build unique, customisable and actionable experiences that automate multiple steps in a workflow.

For this reason, Sisense has a growing presence in the business intelligence and data analytics market. Concurrently to it's growing

---

systems. By using APIs, companies can share their application data and functionality with external third-party developers, business partners, and internal departments within their organisation. APIs include definitions and protocols that help businesses connect different applications they use in their daily operations. This helps save time for employees and breaks down barriers that hinder collaboration and innovation. For developers, API documentation provides a simple way to integrate applications by providing an interface for communication between them.

[67] Sisense - Build intelligent analytics into your products

market share, the advantage is that the tool provides a user-friendly interface, fast performance, and strong data preparation capabilities. The downside is that some users find the visualisation customisation options limited, and the cost can be a concern for smaller organisations.

DUNBAS BI

Dundas Bi is a business intelligence tool developed by Dundas[68], a leading software company, with a focus on reporting and analytics. It is now part of Insightsoftware's Logi Symphony[69], – a leading provider of reporting, analytics, and enterprise performance management software. The tool is designed for Product Managers who are struggling to bring their reporting and analytics vision to life. Dundas Bi holds a notable market share, particularly in the reporting and analytics domain.

The advantage of choosing Dundas Bi is that it offers a comprehensive suite of reporting and analytics features, including data visualisation and self-service capabilities. It offers benefits for anyone who is: (1) stuck delivering poor quality data visualisation content; (2) having inaccessible/inaccurate data with little insights; or (3) users demand consistent user experience. The disadvantages also include the learning curve that may be steep for non-technical users, and the interface can feel overwhelming for beginners.

---

[68] Dundas BI Support

[69] Logi Symphony - Packaged For Every Stage of Analytics Maturity (insightsoftware.com)

ADAPTIVE INSIGHTS

Adaptive Insights, now a part of Workday, was founded in 2003 and offers a cloud-based corporate performance management platform. Adaptive Insights Business Planning Cloud has become the single planning solution moving forward for all Workday customers. This strategy ensures that Workday is offering customers the best solution to accelerate their finance, workforce, and business transformations.

The disadvantage is that you must be part of the Workday ecosystem to benefit from this tool. Another disadvantage is it is primarily focused on financial data, and advanced customisation options may be limited. Despite these limitations, Adaptive Insights specializes in financial planning and forecasting, with integrated data visualisation capabilities. It might be the reason why Adaptive Insights has gained a significant presence in the financial planning and analytics market.

ANALYTICS

Analytics is a cloud-based analytics platform that provides self-service data exploration and visualisation. Analytics has been steadily growing in the analytics market, targeting both small and large enterprises. The advantage is that it offers a user-friendly interface, natural language querying, and AI-driven insights. It emphasises collaboration and sharing. The disadvantage is that advanced analytics features may be limited, and some users may find the pricing higher compared to similar tools.

PLOTLY

Plotly is an open-source data visualisation library that originated in 2012 and has since grown in popularity. As an open-source library, Plotly has a strong community following and is widely used in the data science and programming community. Plotly introduced web-based data visualisation to Python. Today, the company offers Dash Enterprise, which provides the best software tools and platform to enable every enterprise in the world to build and scale data applications quickly and easily.

The advantage of choosing Plotly is that it provides a versatile and interactive library for creating visualisations in various programming languages. It offers customisation and embedding options. The disadvantage is that it requires programming skills to leverage its full potential, and it may not be as user-friendly as dedicated tools.

PYTHON

Python[70] is a popular general-purpose programming language that gained traction in the data science community due to its rich ecosystem of data visualisation libraries. Python lets you work quickly and integrate systems more effectively. For this reason, Python has a significant market share in the data science and analytics community, owing to its versatility and extensive library support.

[70] Welcome to Python.org

The advantage of using Python is that it provides a wide range of libraries such as Matplotlib, Seaborn, and Plotly, allowing for extensive customisation and flexibility in data visualisation. The disadvantage is that Python requires programming skills and may have a steeper learning curve for beginners compared to GUI-based tools.

KEY TAKEAWAYS

In the ever-expanding landscape of data visualisation tools, each option brings its unique advantages and disadvantages. Data visualisation will continue to play a vital role in transforming complex data into easily understandable and actionable insights. Tableau and Power BI dominate the market share, catering to a wide range of users, from beginners to advanced analysts. Excel remains a go-to choice for basic visualisations, while Python and Plotly offer flexibility and customisation for data scientists. MicroStrategy, QlikQ, Looker, Sisense, Dunbas Bi, Adaptive Insights, and Analytics cater to specific business needs.

Ultimately, the choice of a data visualisation tool depends on factors such as budget, user expertise, scalability requirements, and the complexity of the data analysis tasks at hand. Chapter 9 provided a comprehensive comparison of twelve popular data visualisation tools.

What is crucial to remember from the chapter is that:

- **Microsoft Excel**: Excel has evolved to include data visualisation capabilities through Power Pivot, Power View, and Power Query. It offers basic charting and visualisation options suitable for simple data analysis tasks but may be limited in handling large datasets and advanced visualisation functionalities.
- **Tableau**: Tableau gained popularity for its intuitive drag-and-drop interface, powerful analytics capabilities, and

wide range of visualisations. It provides robust features for data exploration and storytelling but may be expensive for small businesses.

- **Power BI**: Developed by Microsoft, Power BI offers excellent integration capabilities, a user-friendly interface, and a broad range of data connectors. It provides strong collaboration features and has gained significant market share due to its association with the Microsoft ecosystem.
- **MicroStrategy**: MicroStrategy offers robust enterprise-grade analytics capabilities, scalability, and security features. However, it may be complex to set up and requires technical expertise, making the learning curve steep for non-technical users.
- **Qlik**: Qlik is known for its associative data indexing technology, powerful data exploration capabilities, and associative search. It provides a seamless user experience but may have a less intuitive interface and be expensive for small businesses.
- **Looker**: Looker, acquired by Google, offers cloud-based data platforms and embedded analytics capabilities. It focuses on collaboration, sharing, and embedding data visualisations. Some users may find the learning curve steep and the interface less intuitive.
- **Sisense**: Sisense is easy to use and scalable, providing AI-driven analytics and seamless integration into existing tech stacks. It offers fast performance and strong data preparation capabilities but may have limited visualisation customisation options and can be costly for smaller organisations.

- **Dundas Bi**: Dundas Bi is a comprehensive reporting and analytics tool with a focus on enterprise-grade capabilities. It offers benefits for users seeking high-quality data visualisation content and consistent user experiences. However, the learning curve may be steep for non-technical users.
- **Adaptive Insights**: Now part of Workday, Adaptive Insights specialises in financial planning and forecasting. It offers integrated data visualisation capabilities but is primarily focused on financial data and may have limited customisation options.
- **Analytics**: Analytics is a cloud-based platform with a user-friendly interface, natural language querying, and AI-driven insights. It emphasises collaboration and sharing, but some users may find the pricing higher compared to similar tools.
- Plotly: Plotly is an open-source data visualisation library widely used in the data science and programming community. It provides versatile and interactive visualisations but requires programming skills and may not be as user-friendly as dedicated tools.
- **Python**: Python is a popular programming language with extensive library support for data visualisation (e.g., Matplotlib, Seaborn, and Plotly). It offers flexibility and customisation options for data scientists but requires programming skills and has a steeper learning curve for beginners.

In conclusion, data visualisation tools offer various advantages and disadvantages, catering to different user needs, budgets, and complexity of data analysis tasks. Tableau and Power BI dominate the market share, while Excel remains a popular choice for basic visualisations. Python and Plotly are popular among data scientists for their flexibility and customisation options. Ultimately, the choice of a data visualisation tool depends on individual requirements and preferences.

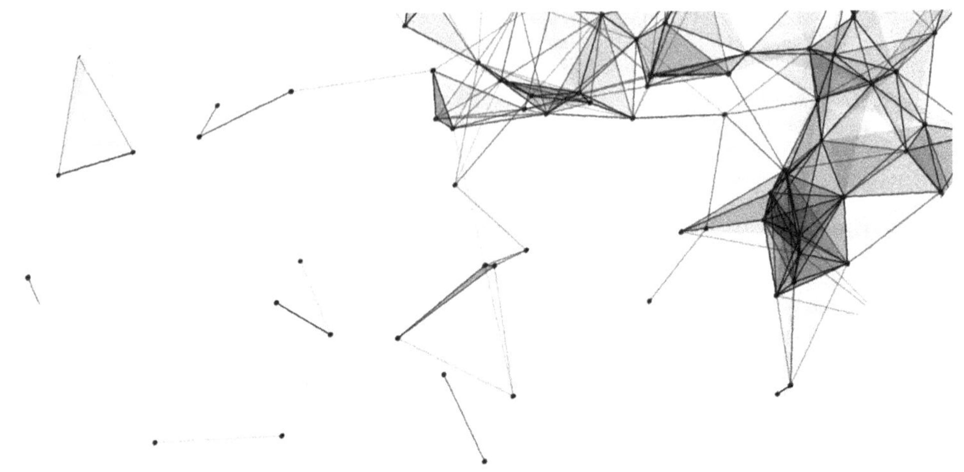

chapter 10

MANAGING YOURSELF FOR SUCCESS – UNLEASHING YOUR POTENTIAL IN THE KNOWLEDGE ECONOMY

In today's rapidly evolving knowledge economy, success hinges on self-awareness and the ability to leverage one's strengths effectively. As a senior analyst with valuable insights and two decades of experience, I aim to guide everyone - predominately women aged between 25 and 45 who are pursuing careers in analysis or considering further studies. Why women you might ask, it is because I have two daughters and a wife who might find this insightful. On the contrary, I am in no way saying that my son is less important.

By addressing important questions, we often ask ourselves about strengths, performance, learning styles, values, and relationships, this chapter aims to empower readers to excel in their chosen paths. I am passionate about anyone who wants to pursue an analyst career as much as I am and about individuals planning to further their studies. This chapter is left for last by design and is broader than my passion or calling. With this in mind, please reflect on the things you love the most about yourself because this might be the key to Being a Valuable Analyst.

WHAT ARE MY STRENGTHS?

I have often expected someone to answer this question for me. This is the wrong way of going about it. Understanding our strengths is a crucial step towards achieving excellence especially if we want to be in analytics. Recognise that building upon existing strengths is more effective than focusing solely on improving weaknesses. Identify the skills and qualities that set you apart and invest your energy in refining and expanding upon them. Finding a band to assist you might be easier. In my case, we as a band scheduled weekly sessions every Friday afternoon to discuss our strengths with each other. By doing these sessions diligently, we finally embraced continuous growth and strive for first-rate performance, which propels us towards excellence. Knowing our strengths helped us improve our performance.

HOW DO I PERFORM?

My suggestion is that rather than attempting to change who you are fundamentally, concentrate on improving the way you perform. This is a bit tricky if you are still in your early 20s because you may not yet have enough experience. It helps to reflect on your work methods, routines, and habits to identify areas for enhancement. Things fell into place for me, as soon as I started to notice a pattern and preferred ways of working. I experimented with different approaches, tools, and techniques to optimize productivity and output. You could do the same too. Seek feedback from mentors, colleagues, and trusted advisors to gain valuable insights into your performance and areas of improvement. People love to talk. It is better to give them a reason to talk. To talk about you in your face and give constructive feedback.

AM I A READER OR A LISTENER?

Understanding your preferred mode of receiving information is vital for efficient learning and effective communication. Some individuals excel as readers, while others thrive as listeners. We all would like to think that we are both, but studies have shown us that you rarely become both. Identify which medium resonates with you the most and tailor learning and communication strategies accordingly. It became a game changer knowing that I was a reader much better than a listener. You are more likely to see me read than being on the radio, talk radio that is. Knowing this allowed me to earn as many university degrees as I wanted. Leverage your preferred style to absorb knowledge, collaborate effectively, and convey ideas. If you are a listener, there are webinars/seminars you can attend to learn your way.

HOW DO I LEARN?

Learning is a lifelong journey, and discovering how we learn best will accelerate our growth. I was told to reflect on whether am I a visual learner who benefits from diagrams and images or perhaps I grasp concepts more easily through hands-on experiences. This reflection is timeless and I suggest you reflect on it too. Understanding your learning style enables you to seek out opportunities, resources, and environments that align with your preferences.

Imagine that interview question, yes, the one about your lack of experience. What would you say now that you realised that you are a visual learner and not a hands-on experience type of person? Now you can finally start applying for jobs outside your experience range. Embrace diverse learning methods to expand your knowledge and develop new skills. Show this when you speak to anyone, even in interviews. It is not bragging, just letting people know that you are awesome. Being awesome should be what you value.

WHAT ARE MY VALUES?

Defining your core values is essential for aligning your career choices with your convictions. There will be times at work when you are rewarded for behaviour that is unsettling to you. Those nights become long as you can't turn back the hands of time.

Reflect on what matters most to you and the impact you want to make through your work. I am not saying go open an NPO (Non-Profit Organisation) to help the needy, No. We should rather consider the values of the organisations we engage with and seek environments that resonate with our principles. When values align with professional pursuits, we will find greater fulfilment and purpose in our careers. We will finally belong.

WHERE DO I BELONG?

Finding a sense of belonging is crucial for career satisfaction and growth. Explore different professional communities, networks, and organisations to identify those that align with your aspirations and values. Sometimes you might be the odd one who finds value in these communities. Don't feel discouraged. Every year I used to walk to the Sandton Convention Centre for our yearly Finance Indaba[71]. I would leave charted accountants at work working on variance analysis as I attended both days.

Don't hold back, engage in industry events, conferences, and online forums to connect with like-minded individuals and expand your network. Some conferences to attend has been listed on the topic

Attending Masterclasses in chapter 2. You are not your team the same way you are not your family. There are more of you outside

[71] Finance Indaba: the biggest finance conference in Africa · CFO South Africa - The annual Finance Indaba is the biggest gathering of finance professionals in the Southern Hemisphere, widely regarded as the best finance conference in Africa since its inception in 2016. Taking place at the Sandton Convention Centre, Finance Indaba promises world-class speakers, live engagement, as well as a complete overview of the tools and services finance teams need to excel in current and future business landscapes.

of your immediate circle. Seek mentorship and collaboration opportunities to foster meaningful relationships and tap into a supportive ecosystem. Lift others out of the mud and change the mindset about how women never look out for each other.

WHAT SHOULD I CONTRIBUTE?

Lift others as you rise. Yes, this is not just a former motto for the Black Management Forum (BMF)[72] but a value we can all aspire to. Identifying your unique contributions is key to making a lasting impact. Consider your strengths, values, and expertise to determine how you can best serve others and contribute to your field. Strive to create value through your work, whether it's by solving complex problems, providing innovative insights, or championing important causes. My sponsor made me aware that I should start where I have control. It was only then that I realised how my former high school, despite being in town, doesn't have an official website. By focusing on making meaningful contributions, I gained fulfilment and established myself as a respected professional. All it took was a visit to the school and I started a mentoring programme and we are working with others to upgrade the IT systems.

RESPONSIBILITY FOR RELATIONSHIPS

In the knowledge economy, success is rarely achieved alone. I have mentioned above how my conversation with a sponsor

[72] BMF - About Us (bmfonline.co.za) - The BMF vision is to be the foremost organisation in the development of managerial leadership and the advancing of socio-economic transformation in South Africa and beyond.

(someone) resulted in me speaking with the school (someone) and we are working on (with someone) upgrading IT systems. Building effective relationships with colleagues, collaborators, and mentors is vital for achieving collective goals. Take the time to understand the strengths and perspectives of the people you work with and learn to leverage them. Once they do great things with them, go and recommend their work (lift as you rise) to someone else. Either verbally, LinkedIn, or whatsoever way seems easier for you. Foster open communication, respect diverse viewpoints, and embrace collaboration to harness the collective power of your team. By cultivating strong relationships, you can enhance your effectiveness and create a supportive network.

REFLECT ON YOUR PATH: RESILIENCE TO PURPOSE

The idea of change, a fresh beginning, or an abrupt turn can make anyone quiver in their boots. And for me, this wasn't just some fleeting fear, but a deep-rooted dread that seemed as familiar as my heartbeat. A flashback from 1998 takes me back to a classroom where I, an ambitious student, was made to swallow the bitter pill of redundancy and forced to repeat a grade. At that moment, I felt robbed of my potential, my confidence, and my vision of being the extraordinary whizz-kid in the room. But time, as they say, has a habit of teaching and healing, and looking back now, the spectre of starting anew no longer haunts me as it once did.

RESILIENCE THROUGH CHANGE AND RESTART

My journey through life has been punctuated by several rest stops and detours. Some were unplanned roadblocks, while others were consciously chosen paths, each bearing their brand of wisdom. Among the involuntary detours, I remember my parents' divorce in 1996 and the subsequent eviction from our family home, a story that echoes with pain and resilience. Then there were decisions of my choosing – starting a family, embarking on a career in banking, and dedicating years to higher studies.

CORPORATE CAMOUFLAGE AND THE ART OF CHANGE

The corporate ladder, with its endless rungs, is often climbed using some tactful strategies. I too attempted to master these, but to my dismay, they yielded nothing. Perhaps we're all reading from the same playbook, becoming suspicious of one another's ambitions. But amidst coffee breaks and idle chats, I found a silver lining. A decision to educate me further, a newfound commitment to knowledge-sharing sessions, and a realisation of the need to evolve – all these seeds were sown during those informal, caffeine-infused chats.

THE CALL FOR CHANGE: A COMMON MELODY

The urge to evolve and advance isn't an isolated sentiment. Many of my colleagues echoed the same yearning, desiring not just hollow titles but meaningful progress. Some of us, perhaps still nursing wounds from our past, feel the need for change acutely.

Those scars, like my own experience of repeating a grade, fuelled my resilience and motivated me to seek out new beginnings. The path may be riddled with uncertainties, but even they are less daunting than a life devoid of progress.

REFLECTION AND GROWTH

I'm far from perfect. I have a strong belief in continual learning, a fact evident from my recent enrolment in a director course. However, this journey of self-evolution isn't a quick fix as some resources might suggest. It's a long-term commitment that demands time, patience, and dedication. Most of the mentors I met lacked the context to truly understand my struggles – a young, determined professional from a disadvantaged background trying to make his mark. Their advice, while insightful, didn't exactly address my situation.

TALKING AND SHARING

"Being An Analyst" was a project I initiated in 2020, aiming to guide others on their career paths. A suggestion from my wife led me to a YouTube[73] channel where I could reach a wider audience. Now that small step has evolved not only into this book but also as a blog[74], a small business, bi-weekly newsletter on LinkedIn called Weekly Analyst[75] and a WhatsApp community page[76]. The journey wasn't smooth; I made mistakes, learned lessons, and refined my

[73] Being An Analyst - YouTube

[74] Being an Analyst Blog

[75] Subscribe on LinkedIn https://www.linkedin.com/build-relation/newsletter-follow?entityUrn=7079076055424094208

[76] WhatsApp Community: https://chat.whatsapp.com/DGOIkliq72Y8Hlr9OzzFJP

approach. Over time, I realised the crux of my mission: to aid individuals in making significant life transitions. I reflected on this when I made a video to share with the top management (Exco) and the rest of the bank's 34,000 employees on the intranet site. It was my first time stating my purpose out loud. Despite reading countless books about how to craft a perfect life purpose statement. On that day, between me and the camera, the truth finally came alive.

My purpose was to share information with information-deprived individuals, not only information but the necessary steps needed for one to get started.

I know this approach is not ideal for everyone and I'm glad that you are part of the journey. I hope this book has helped you and your book club members get started.

KNOWING YOUR AUDIENCE

The answer was staring me in the face all along. My real task was to assist people in changing their course, not merely helping high schoolers choose a path. When I analysed my YouTube viewership, I realised my core audience was primarily working professionals aged 24-45. LinkedIn further confirmed the information about my audience and now with job titles and level of seniority. Armed with this information, I found a new direction and purpose in my work. It is better to have a small target market and focus on all their needs than writing to millions of faceless people.

MY FINAL THOUGHTS

Back in 1995, the thought of change was terrifying. The sting of having to repeat a grade stayed with me, making me wary of radical change. I poured over the advice of so-called 'corporate chameleons', only to find that their guidance didn't apply to my situation. But as I navigated my career and started "Being An Analyst", I realised that the real conversation we need to have is about making significant leaps in our lives. The audience I had attracted mirrored my corporate colleagues, and they too were looking for advice on how to shake things up. If I can help these individuals see things from a new perspective and gather the courage to make their "jump", then I'll have made a meaningful impact.

We have discovered that in today's rapidly evolving knowledge economy, success hinges on self-awareness and the ability to leverage one's strengths effectively. Managing oneself in the knowledge economy requires a deep understanding of (1) strengths, (2) performance preferences, (3) learning styles, (4) values, and (5) relationships. By embracing self-awareness and leveraging these insights, anyone - especially women pursuing careers in analysis or contemplating further studies - can unlock their full potential. Remember, success comes not only from knowing yourself but also from applying that knowledge to continuously grow, contribute, and thrive in the dynamic world of the knowledge economy.

KEY TAKEAWAYS

1. **Embrace Self-Awareness for Success**: In today's rapidly evolving knowledge economy, self-awareness is a crucial factor for success. Understanding your strengths, preferences, and values will empower you to excel in your chosen career path.

2. **Guiding Women in Analysis and Studies**: My aim is to guide everyone, particularly women aged 25 to 45, who are pursuing careers in analysis or considering further studies. This is motivated by my personal connections and a desire to empower women in their professional journeys, especially in technical roles like analysis/analyst manager.

3. **Addressing Essential Questions**: This chapter addresses important questions related to strengths, performance, learning styles, values, and relationships. By exploring these questions, you can gain insights that empower you to thrive in your chosen paths.

- **Leverage Strengths for Excellence**: Recognize that building upon your existing strengths is more effective than solely focusing on improving weaknesses. Invest your energy in refining and expanding upon the skills and qualities that set you apart.
- **Improving Performance Techniques**: Instead of trying to fundamentally change who you are, concentrate on improving the way you perform. Reflect on your work methods, routines, and habits to identify areas for

enhancement. Experiment with different approaches to optimise productivity and output.

- **Understanding Learning Preferences**: Identify whether you excel as a reader or a listener in terms of receiving information. Tailor your learning and communication strategies according to your preferred mode of absorbing knowledge. Leverage your learning style to expand your skills and enhance your learning journey.
- **Aligning with Core Values**: Define your core values to align your career choices with your personal convictions. Reflect on what matters most to you and seek environments that resonate with your principles. When your values align with your professional pursuits, you will find greater fulfilment and purpose in your career.
- **Seeking Belonging and Connection**: Finding a sense of belonging is essential for career satisfaction and growth. Engage in professional communities, networks, and organisations that align with your aspirations and values. Seek mentorship and collaboration opportunities to foster meaningful relationships and tap into a supportive ecosystem.

4. **Making Meaningful Contributions**: Contribute to your field by leveraging your strengths, values, and expertise. Strive to create value through your work, whether it's by solving complex problems, providing innovative insights, or championing important causes. Lift others as you rise and make a lasting impact.

5. **Fostering Relationships for Success**: Success in the knowledge economy rarely happens in isolation. Build effective relationships with colleagues, collaborators, and mentors to

achieve collective goals. Foster open communication, respect diverse viewpoints, and embrace collaboration to harness the power of teamwork.

6. **Resilience Through Change**: Embrace change and new beginnings as part of your journey. Reflect on personal experiences and hardships to fuel your resilience and motivate yourself to seek new opportunities for growth and progress.

7. **The Journey of Self-Evolution**: Continuous learning and self-evolution demand commitment, time, and dedication. Embrace learning opportunities and seek advice from mentors who understand your unique challenges and aspirations.

8. **Empowerment Through Sharing**: My journey of creating "Being An Analyst" underscores the importance of sharing knowledge and experiences to empower others. Small steps can lead to significant impact, and a clear sense of purpose can drive meaningful contributions.

9. **Knowing Your Audience**: Tailor your efforts to cater to a specific target audience. Recognize who benefits most from your guidance and focus on their needs and aspirations.

10. **Making Significant Leaps**: Success in the knowledge economy requires making significant leaps and changes. Empower individuals to see new perspectives and gather the courage to take the necessary steps toward progress and growth.

11. **Unlocking Full Potential**: By embracing self-awareness and leveraging insights related to strengths, preferences, learning

styles, values, and relationships, individuals, especially women pursuing careers in analysis or further studies, can unlock their full potential in the dynamic world of the knowledge economy.

WHATS NEXT?

This section is specifically for you. I have done my best to motivate you to realize that becoming an analyst is an achievable goal. What will set you apart from others is your reason for wanting to become an analyst. I hope you understand the information arbitrage that currently exists between analyst teams and top management. Ninety-six percent of all the information you have about organizational issues and opportunities is unknown to decision-makers. Let us remember the "iceberg of ignorance" concept shared at the beginning of the book.

THE ICEBERG ILLUSTRATION

This shows Top Management being above the waterline and knowing about 4% of the problems with 96% of organisational problems unknown.

Below the Waterline we get (1) Middle Management - knowing about 9% of the problems, (2) Supervisors or Team Leaders - knowing about 74% of the problems, and (3) Front-line Employees who are credited in knowing about 100% of the problems.

I want you to join me today in serving top management with insights. I have benefited, for over a decade, as the analyst manager who supplied insights to top management in the cluster.

There is room for all of us in management offsites. Various tactics can be used to ensure that the executive or management team knows your name and the value you bring to the organization. These tactics may vary based on the situation, so I suggest either a group webinar or a private session. I will post details on all free or paid sessions using these channels.

You can reach out to me by making use of the below details

- Email: info@BeingAnAnalyst.co.za
- LinkedIn: https://www.linkedin.com/in/lisema/

Alternatively, you could follow/subscribe using the below details

- Blog: https://blog.beingananalyst.co.za/
- Weekly Analyst Newsletter: https://www.linkedin.com/build-relation/newsletter-follow?entityUrn=7079076055424094208
- YouTube: https://www.youtube.com/@BeingAnAnalyst
- WhatsApp Community: https://chat.whatsapp.com/DGOIkliq72Y8HIr9OzzFJP

I would urge you to do the following:

1. REFLECT ON KEY TAKEAWAYS

Take some time to reflect on the key insights and lessons you've gained from the book. Consider how they relate to your career aspirations and personal development goals.

2. **SET CLEAR GOALS**

Define your specific goals as an analyst. What type of analyst do you want to be? What industries or sectors interest you the most? Setting clear, achievable goals is essential for career planning.

3. **CREATE A PERSONAL DEVELOPMENT PLAN**

Based on your goals, create a structured plan for your personal and professional development. Identify the skills, knowledge, and experiences you need to acquire or improve to reach your objectives.

4. **NETWORKING**

Networking is crucial in the world of analysis. Start building or expanding your professional network. Attend industry events, join online forums, Being An Analyst webinars, or groups related to data analysis, and connect with professionals in the field.

5. **CONTINUE LEARNING**

Learning is a lifelong journey. This is why I constantly share on the Weekly Analyst Newsletter - which is a free online training and university programmes for your convenience. Please stay updated with the latest trends, tools, and technologies in the field of analysis. Consider enrolling in these courses, attending workshops, or pursuing advanced degrees if they align with your goals.

6. **GAIN PRACTICAL EXPERIENCE**

Practical experience is invaluable. Especially if you want to pursue a different role in analysis. Look for job secondment, vacancies, or projects that allow you to apply what you've learned. Real-world experience can help solidify your skills and make you more attractive to employers.

7. SEEK MENTORSHIP

Find a mentor in the field who can provide guidance, share insights, and help you navigate your career path. Experienced mentors can be instrumental in your professional development. Feel free and reach out to me if you are battling to find a mentor.

8. START OR UPDATE YOUR PORTFOLIO

If relevant to your field of analysis, consider creating a portfolio showcasing your work, projects, or analyses. A well-maintained portfolio can demonstrate your skills to potential employers.

9. STAY INFORMED & ADAPTABLE

Follow thought leaders and influencers in the field on social media to stay informed about industry developments. The field of data analysis is continually evolving. Be adaptable and open to learning new tools and techniques as they emerge. Being flexible and staying current is essential for long-term success.

10. EVALUATE YOUR PROGRESS

Regularly assess your progress toward your goals. Adjust your plan as needed and celebrate your achievements along the way.

Remember that everyone's journey in the field of analysis is unique. Keep your motivation high, stay persistent, and continue to invest in your professional growth as you pursue a successful career as an analyst.

About the Author

Lisema Matsietsi is the visionary founder of 'Being An Analyst,' a community dedicated to cultivating the next generation of analysts. With almost two decades of invaluable experience in the banking industry, Lisema has not only interpreted but also actively shaped strategic narratives within top-tier management boardrooms and strategy sessions.

By mastering the art of intelligent financial reporting, he has consistently acted as a catalyst for transformative change, making substantial contributions towards the achievement of organisational goals.

"My life purpose is to share information with information-deprived individuals which includes the necessary steps to be taken before one could proceed" – **Lisema Matsietsi.**

His mission is crystal clear: to empower aspiring analysts with the indispensable skills and knowledge needed to address the formidable 'Iceberg of Ignorance' – the often unseen 96% of organisational challenges. Through his insightful guidance and the power of analysis, small and medium-sized enterprises (SMMEs) have navigated complex decision-making landscapes with precision, unlocking new vistas of growth and opportunity.

www.ingramcontent.com/pod-product-compliance
Lightning Source LLC
Chambersburg PA
CBHW020154200326
41521CB00006B/362

* 9 7 8 1 7 7 6 4 3 2 1 8 9 *